From Tammy Ellis 6/24/07
Student from
Cody, Wy
(1320 31st St.)
(#3, #5, #7, #9, #10,
helped w. 11 + 12)

Stories from the Living Room

GOOD CATCH
PUBLISHING

This book was written for the express purpose of conveying the love and mercy of Jesus
Christ. The statements in this book are substantially true; however, names and minor
details have been changed to protect people and situations from accusation or incrimi-
nation.

Cover photo by Anthony McConnell

Published in Beaverton, Oregon, by Good Catch Publishing.
www.goodcatchpublishing.com
V1.1

Printed in the United States of America

TABLE OF CONTENTS

	Introduction	9
	Thank You	11
1	I'm Alive	13
2	Eleven Beautiful Babies	21
3	Who Am I?	27
4	Alone	41
5	More of You, Less of Me	47
6	Hidden From The Shadow	57
7	A Wagon Tale	65
8	Little Miracles	75
9	The Love of My Father	81
10	Caught	93
11	Dead Girl Running	103
12	A Good Father	119
13	Growing Pains	129
14	Reality Bites	135

Introduction

Have you ever been sitting around talking with friends and, during your conversation, discovered information that both surprised you and made you appreciate your friends even more? This book is filled with stories like that. These are all real life experiences of people you might know. As you read this book you will recognize the depth of challenging circumstances that many people have gone through. They may even sound remarkably familiar to your own experiences. You'll be inspired to hope in God's ability to help you persevere even in the most difficult of circumstances. You will discover that God is real and really does want to give you a future and a hope.

Thank You

Thanks to all the people who have bravely and humbly told their stories, and to those who listened and worked to write them so we could all be inspired to hope in God. Thanks also to our friends at Good Catch Publishing who worked to help us get this book together. Thanks to the living God, Jesus Christ, without whom we would have no stories to tell.

1

I'M ALIVE!

On a night just like any other, Lori had just gone to bed. The house was dark and her husband and three small children were asleep. As she lay there trying to go to sleep, a suffocating darkness crept into the room and filled every inch of it. The fear of death that she had been tormented with since she was a child had come calling once again, and this time it was more threatening than ever. No longer was she just in fear for her own life, but for the lives of her husband and children as well. She was almost unable to breathe as this feeling of fear and impending doom gripped her with such force that she didn't know if she would survive. She lay there sobbing so hard the bed shook. Her thoughts were flying everywhere, she was sure she had come face to face with the presence of death. She was tormented with the cruel fact that sooner or later she would die, and so would those she loved so dearly. Someday, maybe even soon, they would have to say goodbye.... FOREVER!

Lori imagined herself laying on her deathbed being forced to say goodbye to her children, longing so much to stay and see them grow up. The children were crying and clinging to her hands, while death wrapped its clutches around her body. She felt as though she was being pulled into a deep, dark abyss that had one purpose and one purpose only.... to swallow up its victims and cast them into cold, total blackness never to see the light of day again.

Then, just as she thought she could take no more, the dark presence vanished and an all-encompassing peace took its place -- filling the room and her heart with the assurance that everything was going to be all right. So complete and deep was this peace that she thought, "I could die right now, and I'm not afraid. This must be God!" Lori stopped crying and lay there in total amazement. If she had doubted the existence of God before, she could no longer. She had just experienced the miraculous and she knew it. She wanted this feeling to last forever. She drifted off to sleep with a peaceful smile on her face.

Ever since she had Rheumatic Fever at the age of eleven, Lori was convinced she would die SOON. Lori had to take antibiotics for several months and was told that the illness might have caused damage to her heart. Lori was consumed with fear and soon her fear gave way to the certain knowledge that she was going to die. Every little pain was a heart attack. Every bruise she got was cancer! An achy back was kidney failure. The prayer she had been taught to say each night, as far back as she could remember, took on new meaning and caused her to shudder with fear:

"Now I lay me down to sleep,
I pray the Lord my soul to keep.
If I should die before I wake,
I pray the Lord my soul to take."

In her heart of hearts, Lori knew that she would not be alive past her seventeenth year. The carefree days of her childhood were cut short and gave way to days of fear and dread. Lori's parents were drinking and fighting a lot. What started out as a couple of drinks before dinner on Friday night ended up being a weekend long party, only nobody was having much fun. Now along with this chronic illness, she had to deal with the pain of living in a home that seemed to be headed for disaster. Lori felt all alone. Her parents had always made her feel safe and loved, but alcohol had a way of changing this once happy home into a battleground every weekend.

"Mrs. Chandler, this is Sgt. Mills at the police station. We have your fourteen-year-old daughter, Lori, here. We've got her for being a Minor in Possession."

"In possession of what?" she asked.

"Alcohol," said the officer. "And she seems to have taken in quite a bit more than this bottle could hold."

The next morning, bright and early, the interrogation began.

"What on earth were you thinking?!!" Lori's parents growled.

"Well.... I guess I thought if you could do it, then so could I?" she said wincingly, not so sure that this response would go over very big with them. Boy, was she ever right! She was sentenced to cleaning the house for the rest of the day despite her own self-inflicted headache and occasional upheavals from her churning stomach. In her mind, it was like the scene out of "Cinderella" where she piteously slaves away amidst the dust and ashes cleaning the wicked stepmother's house. Her two older brothers were the wicked stepsisters cackling and mocking her as they stood idly by. It was torture, and worst of all, she had brought it all on herself.

For months after that, Lori lived a quiet life of seclusion. Her mother watched her like a hawk. Forgiveness was not something that was given out, it must be earned and the standards for earning it were incredibly high. She never realized the value of being trusted until she violated that trust; she was determined to earn it back. So until she was a high school senior, Lori lived the reformed life. She hung out with the good girls and stayed out of trouble. She had enough trouble at home without adding to it.

"Happy Birthday," sang Lori's family.

Stories from the Living Room

"How does it feel to be eighteen?" asked Mom.

"I never thought I'd make it," said Lori. "I'm not dead. What a relief!"

"That's a silly thing to say," said Mom. "Of course you're not dead. You've got your whole life ahead of you."

Lori decided that as long as she wasn't dead yet, she might as well have fun.

Alcohol and drugs became part of her lifestyle. She partied just as hard as her parents always had. One night, as she began to drift off to sleep after eating several so-called magic brownies, she woke up gasping for air. She thought that she had forgotten how to breathe and panicked that maybe she had overdone it. Was it her imagination or was she on the verge of an overdose? She thought *What am I doing to myself?* But when the sun rose the next morning, the episode was forgotten, and her eat, drink and be merry mentality returned.

By the time Lori got married fear was so much a part of her life that she worried constantly. She worried about the kids coming down with a terminal illness or breaking their necks on the monkey bars at school. She obsessed over the news reports of missing children and wondered if it could happen to her own. Or what if a murderer broke into their homes in the middle of the night and slaughtered them all in their beds? She had read about such things in the newspaper. Needless to say, all this worry was exhausting.

As she grew older, Lori became cynical about life in general. She prayed every night but wasn't really sure to whom. *Maybe believing in God is just something your parents tell you to do to scare you into being good, kind of like Santa Claus and the Easter Bunny,* she thought to herself. Yet something was stirring in her heart, and she couldn't deny the fact that belief in God, whether He was real or not, had helped her through some tough times.

I'm Alive

Lori thought about taking her kids to church. She wanted them to have something to believe in. Sadly, her idea that God could fill the empty hole in her kids gently blew away, like fog on a windy day.

Lori and her family lived next door to a woman they called "the neighbor from hell." She had actually been a church-going person at one time, but changed when she became addicted to meth. Her name was Carol and she feuded constantly with Lori and hated the kids. One afternoon, Lori happened to come out into her front yard while Carol was sitting in hers.

"Hey Lori," called Carol. Lori braced herself for yet another tirade. "Wanna go with me to church sometime?" asked Carol.

Lori was shocked. *Is this the same woman who tried to sick her dog on me a while back?* she wondered. Lori soon found out that Carol had returned to following God. The change in her was patently obvious, and just as patently confusing. What was it that could change a woman from being ugly and vindictive to laughing and full of love?

For the next few weeks, Lori and Carol spent hours chatting. No matter what topic they were discussing, the conversation always seemed to end up being about God. One day when they went for a walk, Carol asked Lori if she had any questions about God. In spite of her embarrassment, Lori asked Carol if Christians were allowed to drink alcohol. Carol very carefully answered, "Well, you can.... but you probably won't want to." Lori thought to herself, *Fat chance of that!* On another day, the conversation worked its way around to the subject of Satan and devil worship.

"I don't know why anyone would want to follow Satan. He's so ugly and scary," said Lori, shuddering in disgust.

Carol responded, "That's what a lot of people

think. They think that if something is a work of the devil that it's got to be ugly and blatantly evil. But the Bible says that Satan can masquerade as an angel of light. His original name is Lucifer, you know, that means 'light'."

"Wow! I just figured he was this red, scaly dude running around with horns and a pitchfork!" Lori laughed.

This was a real eye opener for Lori. She had never heard such a thing, and her curiosity was roused. Even in the midst of all her mixed-up ways, she had always had an ingrained respect for the Bible, and she thought, *Maybe I should find out what else I don't know.*

"What about all the hypocrites in the church? I know people who are completely different on Sunday than they are the rest of the week," Lori stated.

Carol answered, "One time after Jesus was risen from the dead, Jesus was telling Peter how he would follow Him. Peter said, 'What about John?' Jesus told him not to worry about John, and then he said, 'You follow Me.'" Carol continued, "Being a Christian is about following God for yourself, no matter what other people do. Someday, we will stand before God and He will ask us to give an account for ourselves, not for anyone else."

All of this was a lot for Lori to take in, but she was really enjoying these long chats. She could feel the child-like faith that she once had beginning to stir in her heart again.

On a Friday evening as Lori and Carol sat in the drive-thru at Del Taco, Carol asked, "What do you think of all of it?"

"All of what?" Lori asked.

"You know, Jesus and church and all the stuff we've been talking about," said Carol. "Have you thought of asking Jesus into your heart yet?"

At home, later that night, Lori couldn't stop thinking about their conversation. Was there more to God than what she was experiencing? What did she have to lose?

I'm Alive

She found herself kneeling down next to her bed, and she began to pray, "Dear Heavenly Father, I have been praying to You every night since I was a little kid, but I feel like something is still missing. I know I have sinned, and I believe that Jesus died for my sins. Please forgive me, and please send Jesus to live in my heart. Amen." There were no great signs from heaven, nor were there any "warm fuzzies," but something was just different, as time would tell.

Come Sunday morning, a strange thing happened. Lori found herself up early and actually *wanting* to go to church. She and Carol had talked about going to church together that day and taking their kids, so she went next door to find out what time they were leaving, only to find that Carol had gone away for the weekend. Here was the perfect excuse to not go to church, but amazingly Lori was undeterred. She recalled how Carol had quoted to her the words that Jesus had spoken to Peter, "You follow Me." Wow! Already God was giving her His word to help her on her way. She knew something inside her had changed, and that day she decided she would follow Christ no matter what. So she hurried home and got the kids ready for church. She invited her husband to go, but he said no.

Lori had been to church before, of course. When she was little there was almost always a family in the neighborhood that would invite her to go with them on Christmas and Easter. She had attended a neighborhood Bible study for children called "Good News." As a teenager, she had even spent a whole weekend at a youth retreat. But church on that day was different. It went beyond the guitars, drums and keyboard played in the worship service. It even went past the sermon, which actually made sense to her, sort of. The difference was in herself.

"It's amazing what the Lord has done for me," says Lori. "Just as my neighbor, Carol, had said, the desire for the wild life has been replaced with a desire to live the Christian life, which is better by far. In fact, I would say that the Christian life is a great adventure!"

Fear and worry have lost their hold on me. Things that would have sent me into total panic before I became a Christian just don't get to me like they used to. A few years ago I was told that I might have ovarian cancer. My doctor wanted me to have surgery as soon as possible. Due to other minor health problems that I was having at the time, my surgery was cancelled twice. I had to wait for over a month to find out if my once greatest fear would become reality. Yet through it all God gave me His peace. In fact, this was a very precious time for me because God was right there close. It turned out that I didn't have cancer, but if I had I know that God would have seen me through and used it for good. He is the Master at turning our trials into triumphs!

> Life's darkest enemy;
> The Grave — Death!
> Can no longer taunt to steal my breath.
> Because of what my God has done,
> I'll live forever in the light of the Son!

Hallelujah!! I used to live in fear. Now I'm alive in Christ!"

2

Eleven
Beautiful Babies

One of the first things I noticed when I visited Gordon and Lucille for the first time was the row of pictures. They extend from the edge of the fireplace chimney to the far wall of the living/dining room. Eleven adorable babies. Eleven precious faces looking out. Who are they? They are Gordon and Lucille's children, all eleven of them.

Gordon and Lucille were married in 1949. Their oldest child, Jeanne, was born in 1950. Then there was Yvonne, Monte, Michelle, Twila, Sherree, Denisse, Stephen, Gordon Jr., David and Marty.

The year was 1958 and the Ellis family lived near Belfry, Montana. They had a farm but because a hailstorm had destroyed their crop, Gordon was working in Columbus, Montana as a welder in order to take care of his growing family.

Jeanne and Yvonne were the best of friends. They were the two oldest and sisters! They held hands wherever they went. They looked so much alike some people thought they were twins. One of their favorite games was to make Lucille try and guess which one they were. Of course, Mom always knew but that wouldn't be any fun so sometimes she played along and "guessed wrong."

Stories from the Living Room

Jeanne was seven and Yvonne was six. It was Wednesday and they were at school playing together just like they always did. As they walked by the swing with the old wooden seats, it hit Jeanne in the head accidentally – OUCH! The teacher checked her out and she seemed okay. She gave Yvonne and Jeanne some candy and told them not to say anything about the accident. They went on through their ordinary day. The girls rode the bus home from school and when they got home, told their mom about the swing accident. Lucille checked her over, but didn't see any evidence of a problem.

The next day, Jeanne didn't feel well so she stayed home from school. Friday the doctor would be in town so if Jeanne wasn't better by then, Lucille would take her to see him. On Friday morning, the doctor said Jeanne probably had the flu. She didn't have a concussion, although she did have a small knot on her head. He told Lucille it would be good to take her to the hospital in Red Lodge to have her checked. At the hospital they decided to keep her and just watch her for a couple of days.

Friday afternoon about 3:00 the phone rang. Lucille answered it. The hospital was calling and said that Jeanne was unconscious, in a coma, and they were trying to decide whether to take her to Billings or not. They had bored two or three holes in her head to try to relieve the pressure that was growing. Soon it was decided that there was nothing they were going to be able to do, so they kept her in Red Lodge.

It turns out that the hit with the swing had broken a blood vessel in the center of Jeanne's brain. It was an aneurysm, and her whole brain filled up with blood. The doctor said it was almost inevitable that she wouldn't survive. And, if she did, she would have major brain damage and severe physical handicaps.

Lucille got word to Gordon where he was working in Columbus, Montana. He came as quickly as he could, and arrived just in time. Gordon and Lucille's precious oldest child, Jeanne, died about 11:30 that night.

Jeanne died on Friday night. On Sunday morning, Lucille didn't want to go to church. It was too soon for her yet. Then by that evening, Lucille told Gordon that they just had to go that night. She wasn't sure why, but she just knew they had to go to church. They attended the Lutheran church at the time and there was a visiting pastor that evening. Gordon and Lucille didn't know him and he didn't know them, but the sermon he preached was designed specifically for them. It fit their situation exactly. After the service, they met him and told him about Jeanne. He said, "You know, I had a sermon all ready to preach tonight. About 3:00 this afternoon, as I was on the train, the Lord told me to change it. Now I know why."

Gordon remembers, "One of the things I heard people say about our family was that one child wouldn't be missed because we had six others. That is way, way off the truth. Dinnertime was always the worst for me. I would look up and see that empty chair and would come awful close to tearing up."

Lucille tells me that Yvonne was the only one of the children who was really old enough to remember Jeanne. The baby, Stephen, was only eight months old when this happened. Yvonne had a very trying time, she felt so guilty. The teacher had given them candy and told them that everything was going to be all right and they didn't need to say what happened. Lucille thinks that Yvonne believed that if she had told them earlier everything would have been okay. "It wouldn't have made any difference, of course," Lucille said. "I don't know if it would today, but forty-some years ago it wouldn't have."

Gordon and Lucille had six other children to care for. Of course they had lots of questions. There was a funeral to plan and go through and life to be lived. Yet there was this incredible peace through it all. One of the things that helped was that their pastor was a strong, spiritual man. His calls and support gave them so much strength.

Gordon and Lucille say now that they don't know just how they went through this time -- except for one thing. They were both pretty close to the Lord by then and they knew, even though they didn't understand why this had to happen, that God had a reason, so they didn't question Him. He gave them a strength they didn't have. People sometimes fall apart when things like this happen. Yet they were able to help keep other people together. He used Lucille to help support Gordon's parents, who pretty much fell apart. He used this hard time to help them both grow even stronger in their faith and trust in God, which in turn helped others grow in the Lord. People they knew who didn't go to church before, started to go after they saw what happened to Jeanne and what God did for Gordon and Lucille. God used Jeanne's short life and her death to bring other people to Himself.

Gordon and Lucille talk about Jeanne's faith:

One reason we were able to be peaceful through all of this is that about two years before Jeanne's accident we bought a set of children's books with Bible stories and all the parables that Jesus spoke. Jeanne read them and talked about them all the time. We rest in the faith that we know where she is and while we miss her still today, and every day, we know she's with the Lord.

At the end of his prayers each day, Gordon says to God, "Lord, You have my daughter there. Would You give her a big hug? Knowing that she's in the arms of the Lord makes it a lot easier."

Gordon and Lucille express their faith this way: "God gave all of our children to us and He lets us take care of them for a time. Whether the time is seven years

24

or seventy or sometime in between, they belong to Him. God loves our children even more than we do. Everything, including your children, everything you own, everything you touch, everything you see belongs to God."

Gordon & Lucille's faith comes from their belief that each one of us needs to have a real relationship with God so that when something bad happens we will get through it, not fall apart and away from God. Every person needs to know how he or she stands with God. He's going to help you if you ask. And if He has to take anybody's child back home, He's there to help.

Accidents sometimes take children. Sometimes people say that God shouldn't allow such things to happen. God knows what every child's future will be for them. God took Jeannie home and she is safe with Him. And when your loved ones are safe with the Lord, you can't ask for anything better than that.

Gordon and Lucille Ellis live in Cody and have 10 living adult children, 19 grandchildren and 12 great grandchildren.

Trust the Lord and He will
direct your life. You may not
know how until you have
gone through it.

3

Who Am I?

"Come give us a kiss," Mom said, "Daddy and I are going now, but Jack is going to watch you girls."

Nausea climbed from my gut to my throat. I could barely speak, but I whispered, "Mom, can we go to Grandma's, too? Please?"

"Not tonight, Jack has a fun game of Hide-N-Seek planned. Don't you, Jack?"

"Yes, Ma'am," he said, smiling down at Emily and me.

"Yippee!" squealed my little sister, "I want to be the finder. I don't like to hide."

I shivered. "Neither do I."

The instant the door closed and the bolt clicked, Jack took my hand in his. "Come on, Ruby," he said, "let's go hide. Emily, close your eyes and count to one hundred, then come and find us."

"You know she can only count to three," I hissed.

"Yeah," Emily said, " because I'm only three." "When I'm seven, like Ruby, I can count to seven, when I'm sixteen like you I can count to sixteen and when I'm a hundred I can count to a hundred."

"Just count to three over and over, like last time, till we say we're ready," said Jack.

"Okey-dokey, artichokey," Emily giggled. "One-two-three, ready or not, here I come."

Jack glared. "Do you want to play, or not?"

"Yes," she said, covering her eyes with her hands and counting very slowly.

Jack led me up the stairs, to his bedroom and into his closet. I knew the routine. I hated it. He made me perform oral sex on him. I'd choke, gag and cry. A couple of times I even threw up, but he didn't care.

I wished he'd go and live somewhere else. He was Daddy's cousin. His mom drank herself crazy and was put into an asylum. Jack was sent to live with his nearest relatives, but Grandma and Grandpa couldn't handle him so he came to live with us.

I couldn't tell Mom about what Jack was doing. At the time, it seemed like I must be bad or be doing something bad and deserved it. I felt dirty, scared and ashamed. Jack told me I'd better not ever tell or we'd both be in big trouble. He started waking me up in the night, too, and tiptoeing me into his closet. But, finally, I couldn't take it, and the last time he came for me, I screamed, "No! I'm not doing it. Never again! It's nasty and it's bad."

"I won't be your friend anymore," he said.

I covered my head with my blanket. "I don't care!"

And that was that. The degrading perversions ended that night, and like Jack threatened, so did our "friendship." He stopped being nice to me and completely ignored me.

He became overly friendly to Emily though, and I was afraid after I'd refused him he would turn to my little sister. One night Emily tumbled head first down the stairs, ripping one of her ears almost completely off her head and she had to be rushed to the emergency room. Jack just stuttered and acted all nervous. I was certain Emily must've been trying to get away from him when she fell. I blamed myself; I should've told Mom.

I became increasingly uncomfortable at home. Jack's presence kept me rigid and on guard, and I was relieved when he left to join the Air Force.

Then Daddy started pulling unusual and cruel practical jokes. They were very confusing and I didn't know how to take them. Some of them really terrified Emily and me. Daddy was a policeman for a while and one night he came home from work and picked Emily and me up and set us on the couch.

"You girls look so sweet and innocent, in your little jammies, all clean and ready for bed. Were you good girls today?" he asked, unsnapping his pistol from his holster. He pointed the gun straight at us. Then, he shot.

The blow was deafening and we screamed and cried in horror and thought we were dying. I looked up and down Emily's and my bodies for blood or a bullet hole, or something. Daddy just laughed and laughed. Mom rushed in, wide-eyed and frantic. She fell to her knees and wrapped her arms around both of us till she'd comforted and calmed us down. She apologized for Daddy and explained blanks to us. Mom was furious at him for a long time. I didn't feel safe around him anymore.

Another time our whole family was at the lake with family friends and Daddy kept dunking me under the water. I told him to stop it, but he just laughed and called me a baby. One time he held me under so long I thought I was drowning. I couldn't hold my breath one more instant, and I began to inhale. Water surged and burned into my nostrils. Daddy lifted me up and I gasped and sputtered, then he plunged me under again. He just laughed and said, "You're drowning, Ruby! You're drowning!" When I was able to stop choking and catch my breath, I cried and was so angry I screamed at him. Mom heard me and made him leave me alone, but I was real afraid of him after that.

Then things got even weirder. I was over at my best friend, Ruthie Davis' house one afternoon. Her mom was having coffee with some nice, old lady who smiled at me and asked my name. Before I could tell her, Mrs. Davis said, "Oh, she's the little Rhoades' girl from up the road."

I was stunned. At first I didn't understand it, then, I didn't believe it. After I mulled it over for a while, I decided it made perfect sense and that's why my daddy was so mean to me. I didn't belong to him. Mom had lied to me. What was the big secret about my real father? He must be awful. That made me awful, too.

One time several years later, my sister and Grandma were talking and knew that even though I was in the next room, I could hear them clearly. My sister asked Grandma about the picture of the man with Mom. Grandma told her that he was my real dad but then she hid the picture somewhere. After that there were no more questions. I wondered about my father a lot. Why did he leave me? Where was he? Why all the secrecy?

When I was thirteen, we moved away to a suburb of a big city. I was sent to a middle school that had a larger population than my whole hometown. I was miserable and alone, and hated being the new girl. I felt fat and ugly, flawed and unacceptable. I stuck out like some country bumpkin because I didn't dress, look, talk or act like all of the cool and fearless big city kids. I discovered I was very shy and never could break out of it. I wasn't brave enough or good enough to reach out to anyone. I didn't have one friend until I was a senior in high school, except for Yogi, my wonderful mutt, and he couldn't ask me to the prom.

I missed Ruthie, Grandma and Grandpa, and all my friends from my old school and church. I ate lunch alone, walked to school alone, walked home alone. I hated partner projects, like in biology, or team sports in gym class; I felt like I had to apologize to anyone who got stuck with me.

Who am I?

We never did hook up with any church again. During this hollow and lonely time I attempted to seek God on my own, in my Bible, for companionship and guidance, but I didn't understand anything I read. I had received Jesus as my Savior when I was twelve years old, though I wasn't entirely sure what to do from there. I had learned and believed that God is love and God is kind, and I had memorized the Lord's Prayer.

Finally, a platinum blonde girl named Shandy rescued me from my cell of solitude. I was so thrilled to have a friend I didn't care that she was cynical, wild and maybe not the best kind of friend. At that point, I wouldn't have turned anyone down. We were friends for years. In fact, after we graduated, I moved in with her and her boyfriend's best friend became my boyfriend. At nineteen, I lost my virginity.

I learned quickly that it was much easier to just make out and have sex than to try to get to know a guy and build any kind of relationship. Conversation was difficult. Sex was fairly easy, especially if I got drunk first. I felt desired, accepted, even loved.

I went to school and became a dental assistant. I made lots of friends at the office. We went to the bars every weekend or partied at the dentist's beach condo. He let any of us use it whenever we wanted. I started smoking pot, snorting cocaine, and tripping on anything anybody wanted to share. Shandy moved on.

I met Ron when I was twenty-one and took him to the beach condo the first night. On the way, after Ron talked me into it, I went to visit my real father. He had remarried and had five more children. It was pretty uncomfortable and we didn't really delve too deep. I felt good about finally getting to meet him, but he was real quiet, like me, and we just couldn't seem to spark even the smallest conversation. I was disappointed.

Stories from the Living Room

Mom and Daddy found out I contacted my father. My mom told her mom and then came the stories. My grandma would talk about my father returning from the Korean War and running around on Mom all the time. Mom divorced him and went to work in a cannery. The people who babysat me had a son who also returned home from the war, and when he met Mom they fell in love and married. That was Daddy. He harassed my real father out of town and adopted me.

Mom and Daddy discovered I was seeing Ron and that he had moved in with me. Daddy ranted and raved and said he'd kick Ron's butt if he didn't marry me. So, to appease my parents, we married. At first I wanted the role of wife. I tried to be a good homemaker, cooking and cleaning. I even quit going out. Ron didn't, though. It was a one-sided marriage and it got really old, really fast. So, I joined him at the bar and made up for lost time.

We were drunk and stoned all the time. It didn't take me long to acquire a twelve-pack-of-beer-a-day habit; then it got worse. I drank myself into oblivion almost nightly. I didn't know what I was doing or where I had been the night before. I was blacking out and facing huge gaps of time I couldn't account for. One night I woke up in an unfamiliar house and a strange man was on top of me, raping me.

I hated my life; I couldn't stand what I had become. It was no wonder my mind chose blackouts over remembering. I started reading self-help books and articles and began to understand why I made the harmful choices I made. However, I was too entrenched to break the patterns. I drank even more trying to dull the pain of knowing I was in a hole I couldn't climb out of. I used to cry every night and recite the Lord's Prayer; I hoped God could somehow rescue me.

My relationship with Ron was as messed up as we were. I wanted a good marriage, but we had more of a party partnership. Our foundation was not love; our connection was drugs and alcohol. Addiction is not a solid core to build upon. Calling what we had a marriage made us sound pretty together, like we were living the American dream. But the truth was, we had built our lives on a pack of lies and every storm that blew in chipped away at us. Then Ron heard about my rape. He became enraged and accused me of having an affair, because I hadn't told him about it. We got into a huge fight and when he started throwing things, I left.

I went over to a friend's house. I was pretty shaken up, and a man was there who consoled me and we ended up in the sack. That's when my son was conceived. I couldn't say it was Ron's baby because he'd had a vasectomy. I was too terrified to tell him, so I just left, with no explanation, and ended up at my sister's.

For three days I had no distractions, no TV, no phone, no drugs, no alcohol. I was considering having an abortion and I was scared. I knew abortion was wrong, I was just too afraid of facing Ron. I wanted to make it go away. I opened Emily's Bible and began to read. I learned that every child is a gift from God. God causes every single conception; no child is an accident. I reasoned that if I accepted other gifts without destroying them, I should receive *this* gift from God and not destroy it. I kept my baby.

I finally told Ron and he reacted just as I had envisioned. I moved in with my folks and when Terry was born, he was sick and had to be flown to a neonatal clinic. He had lost oxygen for a short time and faced the possibilities of blindness, deafness or being mentally delayed.

Emily told a lady she worked with, Loretta, about Terry. Loretta said her son-in-law was a pastor and she'd have him pray. Unbeknownst to me, many people from Loretta's church began praying for my baby and me. Also, the 700 Club had been notified and a worldwide network of prayers began. A week later, Terry was able to come home. He was declared healthy by his doctors and never suffered any complications.

Terry and I stayed with Mom and Daddy until we got caught in their adult-living mobile home park, then we rented an apartment with Emily. I received state aid and was able to stay home and raise my baby. I wanted to be a good mom and stayed away from the bars. I couldn't afford to go out anyway. But trouble had a way of seeking me out and before long, I became involved with another wayward man and, once again, I was engulfed in addiction and hopelessness.

About this time, Mom went into the hospital to have gallstones removed and when they opened her up, they discovered she was full of cancer. The cancer was malignant and she died seven months later. Two weeks to the day after that, Daddy killed himself.

Though this was a grievous and sorrowful period in my life, God gave me comfort. I wasn't even serving Him at the time, yet He poured out His peace and it surpassed my understanding. I was even able to console my brother and sister with truths from way back in Sunday school that came flooding into my mind. God is love. God is kind. I just knew God was in control and we could trust Him.

I don't know why I couldn't carry that same trust in God into the rest of my life, like when I found myself alone again. My boyfriend left me for another woman. Mom and Daddy were gone. Emily moved out of our apartment and in with her abusive boyfriend. Now, without her half, all the money I received from the state went for rent. It was just my boy and I and a few food stamps. We had nothing and no one else.

I got nervous and I got lonely. I really needed adult companionship, so I went out, not even to party, just to mingle...and in walked Tom. We were in bed that night and he moved in within the week. I welcomed his fat wallet, but he was an explosive man with a short fuse. I was very uneasy about leaving my son alone with him. I had gotten a part-time job as a waitress and imagined the most awful scenarios while I was away. One night we were drunk and I told Tom I didn't like him slapping Terry all the time. He grabbed me by the throat and nearly choked me to death. I fought until I couldn't and felt my strength and life draining out of me. I collapsed to the floor, and he stopped.

A couple named Bobby and Bev moved in next door. Tom worked with Bobby, but didn't like him. "They're Bible-thumpers," he said. I really hit it off with them and whenever Tom was at work, Bev and sometimes Bobby, too, would come over and we'd drink wine, smoke dope and search the Bible together, trying to figure things out.

About that time, Emily got pregnant and moved into a women's shelter to escape her violent boyfriend. A lady named Molly, from the Foursquare Church, was visiting the shelter one day and gave Emily forty dollars. She said, "This money is for you. Don't worry about what you spend it on. Buy whatever you need." Emily was blown away by her kindness and never forgot it. In fact, after she had her baby, she started attending Molly's church. She would swing by and pick Terry up for Sunday school. Then, afterwards, I would feed us all lunch and Emily would recount to me everything she'd learned at this "interactive, fun church where they actually laugh."

One day, Emily asked me if I knew Jesus. I said, "Oh, yes."

She said, "Do you know fornicators won't see the Kingdom of Heaven?"

"No, I don't believe that. God is kind."

Emily showed me Ephesians 5:5 and I started sleeping on the couch. Between my sister and our neighbors, I was being immersed in God's word. Tom was furious.

One summer afternoon I was taking a shower, getting ready for work, when Tom walked in and shouted, "I'm taking the car."

"For how long?" I asked.

"All day."

"I don't think so. I need it for work."

"You can walk."

"That car is in my name, and if you take it, I'll call the cops and report it stolen."

He swiped the shower curtain open, grabbed me by the neck and dragged me out of the tub. I screamed. Every time he'd release enough pressure on my throat to pound on me, I'd scream again. Bev happened to be outside and heard us through the open window. In she marched, a mountain of a woman, and shouted a string of threats and profanities at Tom. He headed for her, at one point, and she said, "Go ahead, little man, make my day. Come on!" He just shoved her out of the way and left...but not with my car. I got a restraining order and after he moved all his belongings out, I didn't see him anymore. Then, I found out I was pregnant.

About this time, I began to feel God's call on my life and started visiting the Foursquare Church Emily was so excited about. I ran into some friends I used to party with, but who had since become Christians. They were so excited that I was not partying and wanted to get straightened out that they wanted to help me in any way they could. They started dropping in on me at home and saw my desperate predicament -- no husband, no parents, a four-year-old child, a baby on the way and no money. Through some connections and some divine favor, they got me accepted into a nice, low-income apartment. That saved me. A very kind man from the church showed up in a beat-up orange van and helped me move.

I continued going to church, though I was still very shy and full of fear. I had a hard time connecting with people. I could meet them and smile, shake hands or even give a hug, but when it came to any type of conversation, I'd just go blank, blush and look down or look around the room. I really wanted relationships, but I had no people skills. My lifestyle never had required much verbal intimacy.

One day I met a warm and wonderful couple named Kenny and Connie. They welcomed Terry and me every Sunday. They accepted us and loved on us in spite of my backward, goony mannerisms. Eventually, I got comfortable with them and advanced past the stuttering, fidgeting, sweating, constant clearing of the throat phase, and got to know them. As it turned out, Kenny was the son-in-law of the Loretta that Emily had worked with. He was the pastor and these were the people that had prayed for Terry when he was born. I couldn't believe it; what a "coincidence!"

I received Jesus as my Savior and Lord of my shaky life in 1985. I pressed past my fear of water and got baptized in Lake Tillicum. I quit drugs, sex and alcohol. I had a difficult time quitting cigarettes, but the Lord actually gave me a plan on how to quit and then gave me the self-control to implement it. I quit smoking while I was pregnant with my daughter.

Angie was born healthy and beautiful. I never, ever regretted having my children. Of all my gifts from God, they are truly the most awesome. I did regret the consequences of my sinful past. The effects reached far beyond just me, they hit my kids, too. They had to grow up without daddies. We had lots of struggles and lots of heartaches.

I was always honest with the kids about my past. I hoped I could save them from the same messes I'd made. I never bashed their dads, as tempting as it was sometimes. I never wanted to burden them with thoughts that they were spawned from evil men. Also, I never wanted them to have a negative father-image; I wanted them to have a great concept of their Heavenly Father, and it worked. They knew God, loved Him and acknowledged Him as the Father in our home, the head of our household.

I never married again. That's all in God's hands. I have gotten lonely for male companionship, and wondered why God didn't ever send some perfect soul mate to me. But it makes me feel kind of special that God wants me all to himself. I actually had a lot of healing to go through. What Jack did to me messed me up; it taught me that if I didn't have sex I wouldn't have friends. That lie was planted when I was a little girl; I believed it and it grew into a whole messed-up belief system of promiscuity. God needed to undo a lot of damage that had been done. He taught me the truth about relationships and opened my eyes to the lies that fueled my unhealthy attractions and addictions.

I had always perceived God as distant and it took a while to trust His constant closeness. Father figures weren't too high on my hero list, so He had to move slowly and tenderly and show me I could trust His fatherhood. He showed me that even when I didn't know or love Him, He always loved me. He had always been faithful to me, even when my back was turned to Him and I was living in the shadow of my sin and shame. Now, He wanted a commitment from me. It was my turn to be faithful to Him. He wanted my full submission and, eventually, I gave it to Him. He taught me deep, sincere intimacy, how to communicate and how to be faithful…never my strong points. I now know I am loved and valuable. What an unparalleled sensation!

God has baby-stepped me from fear and timidity into victorious living. I live a life full of peace and joy. I am free from the shackles of shame that bound me and I tell my story because I love you and I want you to have what I've found. No darkness you are cornered in, no sin you are ensnared by can keep you from God if you are willing to be forgiven and changed. "For I know the thoughts I think towards you," says the Lord, "thoughts of peace and not of evil, to give you a future and a hope. Then you will call upon Me and go and pray to Me and I will listen to you. And you will seek Me and find Me when you search for Me with your whole heart. I will be found by you and I will bring you back from your captivity." (Jeremiah 29:11-14)

I was six years old, it was a stormy night, and there was a bad thunderstorm. I knew I needed Jesus in my life, so I managed to get out of bed and go to my dad. That night my dad told me about Jesus and I accepted Him into my life. Since that time I love thunderstorms.

4

Alone

"I hate them, all of them! They are so wrong! What is their problem? Why can't they act right? Fine, if that's the way they want to be, I'll just be alone! A-L-O-N-E! Alone!" Melissa cried. She quit talking to anyone.

When we lived in California things were fine. We were a happy, church-going family, Dad, Mom and all five kids. Then we moved to Wyoming. I was only six years old when we moved, but I remember how things used to be and how bad it got after we arrived here. Dad worked all the time. Mom stayed home with us kids all day, which stressed her out so much that when Dad got home she'd go out dancing with her friends. Dad would sit home and cry and yet we still went to church.

Then one day when I was in the eighth grade, I came home from school. Mom was sitting at the kitchen table with my younger brother. "Sit down, Melissa, I have something to tell you" Mom said softly. "Some things are going to change, Melissa. I'm going to leave your Dad. I'm going to have another home to live in. I'm hoping you will come and live with me."

My throat tightened and I clenched my teeth as if locked in time. I felt like my chest was going to explode as I sat frozen in the chair. Then I heard myself tell Mom, "Okay."

That day was the saddest of my life. They had forced me to choose. I went with Mom just because she asked. Mom divorced Dad and since I went with Mom, that meant I divorced him too. How could Mom do that to Dad, to us?

I hated my Mom for leaving Dad and marrying David! I thought to myself, *David and his stupid ponytail. He had better look out or I'll grab him by that stupid ponytail, drag him around the house and then cut it off!* I hated David, too!

Now I was the one sitting and crying. I was sure the whole town knew how awful we were. Some great Christians we were – divorced parents, my sister moved back to California to finish high school, my older brothers, the twins, were doing drugs, drinking and just generally being rebellious. My little brother was really out of it. He seemed to think all this was so cool.

They were all wrong! Everything was so wrong!

Life seemed to be such a waste. My Dad wasted his life being sad. He and Mom never talked about anything. No one in this used-to-be-a-family talked. Mom wasted her life too. We used to go to church and be happy, now everything was gone and just a waste. What was the point?

Dad tried to get me to tell him about Mom and David. Mom wanted me to act like everything was great. One time I told Mom I felt like killing myself just to get out of the mess. I don't think I really wanted to die, but I sure did want out of it all. I was so tired of all the pain and sadness. I was sure if things had just stayed like they were in California, we would all have been happy instead of so sad and angry and alone. Seven people in a family (eight if you count that creep, David) and we were all alone. We never talked. We didn't love. We didn't....

There was no hope for us. We were lost. No one went to church. No one loved God. I sure didn't. Why would I? If God loved me, He would never have let my family fall apart like that. I prayed and cried, and He never answered me. He left me all alone.

I was finally out of high school and met the nicest guy. Aaron was a Christian and went to church over in Cody. I didn't intend to go with him, but it was nice that he was such a great guy and really seemed to love me. It was so good to feel love for a change. He was sure a lot happier than anyone in *my* family. Aaron and I were getting more and more involved. We didn't have sex, but we sure did a lot of other physical touching and things I didn't think Christians were supposed to do. But Aaron was so nice and made me feel so loved.

My sister came back from California and was working and living in Cody. She started going to church over there. Some people from her work went to the Foursquare Church and invited her. She really liked it and she invited Aaron and I to come all the time. She kept telling me that what Aaron and I were doing was wrong and I needed to come to church. I didn't think God cared about me so why would I go and pretend to care about Him.

Aaron wanted me to go to some weekend thing at his church. He would be there and it would be a way to spend more time with him and less time at home alone, so why not.

There were about 30 teenagers there for the weekend. That was cool. Too bad I didn't know them and they didn't know me. I was with all those people and alone again. *Oh well*, I thought, *I'll listen to what they have to say*.

It seemed like there were other people who went to church who didn't have such perfect families either. That girl had it pretty bad, worse than me, yet she seemed to love God. Why?

After listening to the speakers and to other teenagers talk about their lives and what Jesus had done for them, I was starting to see that maybe I had been misunderstanding God for a long time. Jesus suffered and died on the cross so I could have life and life more abundantly. Yet my life had not been abundant. So how could all this fit together? Besides, according to everyone who seemed to know God, what I had been doing with Aaron was wrong, and if my thinking was all wrong – God wouldn't accept me anyway. This was confusing!

Sunday morning the guy speaking said we should take our sins and write them on a piece of paper and then take it up front and nail it to the cross. He really had a hammer and nails and wanted us to do it. Hum. Well, what could it hurt? I wanted to feel better that was for sure. If God could help these other people, maybe He would help me, too.

Okay, pen and paper – write! Aaron and our relationship. I had to write that and I probably needed to quit going out with him, but I didn't want to stop seeing him so maybe we could work something out. *God, I believe in You, now I want to believe You. I want to have true peace, joy and love in my life. Take my relationship with Aaron. Here, I nail it to the cross.*

That was the beginning for me. Soon after that weekend I didn't want to stop seeing Aaron, but he broke up with me. That was horrible! I cried out, "God, I thought things were going to get better not worse? I really don't want to go backwards. I'm just starting to come out of the depression I've been in because of my family, now Aaron breaks up with me. How will I ever keep from being so depressed, sad and lonely?"

Then … I heard God talking to me. No, I'm not crazy, I heard Him in my heart of hearts. It must be because He lives inside me that I hear Him talking to me from there. I clearly heard Him say, *Trust Me, Melissa. I do love you. I know the pain you have suffered, I have suffered with you. I have suffered with your Mom and Dad and your sister and brothers, too. I love all of you. Believe me, the divorce and pain your family suffered was not my will, but I have used it, and I will keep on using it. Every time Satan does something destructive to a family, I will step in and restore them if they will let me.*

Well, I have to tell the truth. At first that was really hard for me to believe. I mean to believe it in a way that it would change my thinking. But now I *do* know that God loves me. He died for my sins and He is restoring my family and me.

My Mom and David went through some hard times in their marriage, but I prayed for them and so did others. Mom has rededicated her life to God and David has become a Christian. They are happy and have a good marriage. My Dad just got married and is walking with the Lord again. My sister is walking so close to God and just got married to a wonderful Christian guy. I'm going to the same church she goes to and I live and work in Cody. I have an apartment and I live alone, but I'm not alone anymore, God is always with me and I know it.

If I could tell anyone anything at all right now it is this: "No one has to hide or stay in the place of hurt and pain. I have finally been able to let go of the pain of my past, and you can, too. God has given me the peace and happiness I always thought came from my family being just perfect. Now I know that true joy and peace and real love come from God and His love for me. He wants to do the same for everyone who is hurting because of their past. You just have to get to know Him and let Him love you. It isn't always easy, but it's definitely worth it!"

5

More of You, Less of Me

"Good morning, Lord. Thank You for this day. What shall I wear? My bibs? My jeans? OK, my jeans. I'll have to wear a long T-shirt with them, though, is that all right? My jeans are getting so baggy Mom and Dad will just say something to try to make me eat. Lord, give me the strength to continue to stand against them and their attempts to annihilate our plans…"

"Shannon, breakfast is ready," my brother, Wayne, called.

"See, Lord, it's starting already. What do You want me to do today? Do You want me to fast breakfast? Lunch? Dinner? All day? Just junk food? What? I hate Saturdays. My family just eats and eats and eats all day long…"

"Shannon!" Mom yelled, "Come on!"

"I'm really not all that hungry…"

"Young lady," Dad hollered, "you get down here, now! You look like a scarecrow and you will eat breakfast today. You don't have to indulge in our sinful decadent poisons, but you will eat something, a banana maybe."

"Lord, can I or can't I eat breakfast? A banana would be fine? Thank You, Lord."

"Do I have to come up there?" Dad boomed.

"Coming," I said, cinching my bulky terry cloth robe around my waist. The greasy, smoky stench of fried bacon met me halfway down the stairs. I gagged. "Gross! Lord, forgive them for what they do. Please make them better stewards of their bodies and make them let me be the good steward of mine that You have called me to be."

"There's my sunshine," said Dad, squeezing my shoulder.

"Hi, Daddy."

"Hi, Sweetie," Mom smiled. "Do you want breakfast?"

"Just a banana, please," I said.

Mom plopped the platters of fat, fat, sugar and fat all around the table. I felt my throat close off and wondered if the banana would go down. Dad blessed the empty calories and they all began slurping and smacking and clogging their arteries. I couldn't swallow. I spit my banana into my napkin, while pretending to wipe my mouth.

"Smooth," said Wayne, winking at me.

"So," said Dad, with his mouth full of buttered, jellied, white bread toast, "tomorrow is the big fifteen." He shook his head back and forth, and then flapped his arms like a duck. "How time has flown. You're making me old, kiddo."

"What do you want to do for your birthday, honey?" Mom asked.

"I would love to lay in my room all day long and read this awesome book I just started," I said, wishing immediately that I hadn't mentioned the book.

"That sounds like some celebration," said Wayne, rolling his eyes.

"What book are you reading?" asked Dad.

I hesitated and prayed silently, "Lord, don't let them take my book away..."

"Shannon, what book are you reading? Not one of the ones we agreed you wouldn't read until you're older?" asked Mom.

More of You, Less of Me

"Could you guys lay off? It's a book on fasting, all right? God wants me to read it, and He wants me to fast. Why didn't you ever teach me about fasting? Why do you want to keep me from learning all there is to know about Him? You can't make me stop reading. I will do what God tells me to do, not what you tell me to do. Stop trying to sabotage my relationship with my God!"

"Let me have the book," said Dad. "You are not to help yourself to our books. They are too mature for you. Intelligence-wise you're sharp, but spiritually and emotionally, you're not quite as grown up as you think you are and you are not reading that book. Also, until you put some weight on your bones, the very last thing you will be doing is fasting!"

"Daddy, God has called me to fast," I said, sobbing. "You can't make me eat. You shouldn't even try. God will destroy you if you try to thwart His plans."

"Young lady, I've had about enough..." Dad began.

"Stop it! shouted Mom. "Stop fighting at the table. Shannon, eat your food. Let's change the subject. Why don't we plan something fun for tomorrow, as a family, like going boating in Yellowstone?"

"OK," I said, hoping everyone would forget about my book.

"Then, after we get home, you can invite some of your friends over for cake and ice cream," Mom said.

"Mom, I don't want cake and ice cream."

"Well, I thought maybe a carrot or a zucchini cake would be fine. Please let me make you a birthday cake. I've never not. I'd feel terrible," Mom begged, beginning to cry.

"No cake, no way. Sure, there's a cup of veggies inside, but there's still tons of sugar, butter, eggs, white flour, junk! You know I don't put those toxins..."

"...into your temple. We know," said Wayne.

Stories from the Living Room

"Mom, please stop crying. You can make me a fruit salad...no marshmallows, no Cool Whip. I'll call Joni and Brenda and invite them over. What time?" I knew my friends, rather ex-friends, wouldn't come. We'd brushed each other off months ago, which was for the best; we were totally unequally yoked. I was just trying to cheer Mom up.

"I'm so worried about you, Shannon. I don't know what's happening to you. You are not yourself. You are too thin and you're disrespectful and rebellious. I'm at my wit's end. Talk to me..." Mom sniffled.

"This sucks!" I yelled, crossing my arms and scooting my chair back from the table.

"Shannon, you apologize to your mother!" Dad ordered.

"May I be excused?" I asked.

"Apologize!"

"I'm sorry!"

"You're excused!"

I stomped up to my bedroom and threw myself on my bed. "God, where are You? Is this just my cross to bear? My family? Alone? Please rescue me from this nightmare that is them."

"Knock-knock," said Mom, opening my door.

"I really don't want to talk right now, Mom."

"I know. How about if just you and I go to lunch tomorrow, all by ourselves? We'll go someplace with a nice salad bar."

"Okay, Mom. That sounds wonderful. Look, I'm trying to pray..."

"All right. Lunch then, fruit salad later. Sound good?"

"Yes."

Mom hugged me. "I love you, Shannon."

"I love you too, Mom."

Lunch was a complete disaster. It was just a ploy

to pry inside my head. Mom begged me to tell her what my thoughts were. "Tell me one thing you're thinking so I know where you are."

"I'm thinking it's none of your business. My thoughts are between me and God and you are intruding." I pursed my lips shut and didn't eat or say another word.

"You win, Shannon," said Mom.

The resolute way she said those words frightened me. They echoed through my head all the way home. I felt like a helium balloon that had just been released, abandoned and forgotten, to drift by itself into oblivion.

In my room, I looked at my reflection in a full-length mirror. My eyes protruded from my pale, grayish face like two burnt out light bulbs. The wild nest on my head hadn't been detangled in so long I couldn't even slide my fingers through it, let alone a comb. No make-up, no jewelry, no smile, no sparkle…and the shapes of each of my bones showed right beneath my skin. Was this really what God wanted? What if it wasn't? Not even my mom would try to save me now. "Oh, I'm being ridiculous, forgive me, Lord. Of course this is what You want. More of You and less of me. All those pleasures and luxuries are vanities and prideful excesses. I choose to be Your humble servant." I prayed like I knew what I was doing, but confusion had found a door and blew in like a tsunami.

Mom had home schooled Wayne and me since kindergarten. She worked very hard to tailor the Christian curriculum to meet each of our needs, strengths and interests. I loved school. For a while, I suspected she was trying to infiltrate my thoughts through some of the essay assignments she gave me, but that abruptly stopped. I had succeeded in pushing my mom completely away.

I felt lonely. "Comfort me, Lord…if, if You want me comforted…maybe You don't. I don't know. Whatever Your will is, Lord." I felt dirty. I began washing my hands, obsessively -- compulsively. I tried not to touch anything that would contaminate me. There were so many microscopic pollutants I couldn't even see. I writhed and itched and scratched constantly. I scrubbed with abrasive soap and a fingernail brush until my flesh bled. "Lord, cleanse me. Give me clean hands and a pure heart."

Nobody said anything anymore about my haggard appearance, my strange behaviors or my anorexia. Like Mom said, I won. I scarcely ate. Even a small, dry salad of Romaine lettuce made me feel heavy, bloated and nauseous. I thought God just didn't want me to eat.

Every task took me forever to accomplish. In addition to having zero energy, I was more confused than ever. Mom asked me to clean the bathroom one afternoon, and four hours later she had to come in and make me stop. It wasn't filthy, it just needed wiped down. I didn't know where to stop ... so many germs. I asked God for wisdom during every step of the process, "Lord, should I clean the toilet next? Is this shiny enough? Do I need more bleach? Is it disinfected yet?" I thought because *I* thought it wasn't clean enough that God was telling me it wasn't clean enough.

For nearly two years I followed the directives of the voice in my head. I believed since I was a Christian, my thoughts were God's thoughts. All of them. Whatever entered my mind, I obeyed. Eventually, I lost myself and began cascading down this long, deep, dark abyss. I couldn't stop the fall. It was out of my control. I was out of my control. It had never occurred to me that this might be the devil. After all, I was a child of God, how could Satan deceive me? One night I became completely terrified, disoriented and desperate. I knew in my heart that it was not God who was tormenting me. I lifted my arms to heaven and cried out, "Lord, I need help! If there is anything You can do to save me, please, save me! I'll do anything!"

I was still in the web of confusion, but the very next morning, I found the courage to ask my mom for help. She sobbed and held me so tightly I thought I would snap. We prayed for direction. Both of us felt led to seek my grandma's help. She has a wonderful gift of spiritual discernment. The three of us talked, prayed and cried together. I opened up my mind and heart completely, telling them every single thought I had, no matter how bizarre I knew it would sound to them. We exposed the lies I had believed and replaced them with truths from the word of God. We stormed and battled for two days until finally, I felt some relief. I felt a freeing, a releasing, like I was regaining my sanity. My thoughts were brighter and clearer. Fingers untangled from the gnarl in my mind and I felt like myself again.

Grandma concluded that at some point I had decided that to be holy, I had to self-destruct. To please God I had to destroy myself. I believed deep down, that God was not good. He wanted me to sacrifice everything to Him, and didn't want me to enjoy life or have any pleasure. He wanted me to abstain from all good things.

After Mom and I went home, I went to bed. I was spent. When I awoke, I asked her to cook me bacon and eggs, toast and cocoa. I enjoyed every delicious bite, with no trace of guilt! Before, there would have been tremendous condemnation. I was free! I was overcome with joy; I cried, sang and thanked God for releasing me from captivity. I could actually feel that the bondage was really broken. All the confusion was gone. I was back. I never, ever felt happier or more grateful.

I'm not sure how this deception got started. Maybe it was my isolation. Even Christians need at least a few people to be accountable to. We're all susceptible to error. Maybe when I began disobeying my parents, by reading books they told me not to, I opened a door for

Satan to enter in. I should have been weighing everything against God's word, but there was so much pride involved in my rebellion, I thought I was always right on target.

A couple of days after my extrication from darkness, the old, familiar veil of confusion tried to overshadow me again. I was being plagued by old thought patterns. This time, however, they were fighting for control over me from the outside. They weren't inside me and I determined they *would not* come back in. I did get scared. Doubt taunted my faith. I had to ask my mom, "Wasn't I set free?"

"Yes, you were!" she cried. To help me succeed, she cut out little cards for me and wrote Scripture verses on them for me to recite. On one she wrote: I HAVE BEEN REDEEMED BY JESUS AND I'M NOT GOING TO LET THIS CONFUSION COME BACK! I punched holes in the cards and put them on a chain around my neck. Every time I felt an attack, I'd yank them out and declare God's truth. I knew I was fighting for my freedom, my sanity, my life. I was engaged in spiritual warfare. God's word is the "sword of the Spirit", and using that sword, I fought with all my might. God fought for me with all His might, too, and, again, Satan was defeated! He's never tried his confusion tactics on me since.

When I really got to know God for who He is, instead of the monster I thought He was, I had Jeremiah 29:11 inscribed on my class ring, just as a reminder: "FOR I KNOW THE PLANS I HAVE FOR YOU," SAYS THE LORD. "THEY ARE PLANS FOR GOOD AND NOT FOR DISASTER, TO GIVE YOU A FUTURE AND A HOPE."

God has come through for me in such huge ways. I am so thankful and have such a deep assurance of His reality and His goodness. I called out to Him and He answered, healed, delivered and saved me. When everyone else had concluded there was no way of penetrating my defiant shell, God found a way.

I love Psalm 107, I feel like it was written just for me! "Give thanks to the Lord, for he is good! His faithful love endures forever. Has the LORD redeemed you? Then speak out! Tell others he has saved you from your enemies...Some wandered in the desert, lost and homeless. Hungry and thirsty, they nearly died. 'LORD, help!' they cried in their trouble, and he rescued them from their distress...Some sat in darkness and deepest gloom, miserable prisoners in chains...'LORD, help!' they cried in their trouble, and he saved them from the darkness and deepest gloom; he snapped their chains. Let them praise the LORD for his great love and for all his wonderful deeds to them. For he broke down their prison gates of bronze; he cut apart their bars of iron. Some were fools in their rebellion; they suffered for their sins. Their appetites were gone, and death was near. 'LORD, help!' they cried in their trouble, and he saved them from their distress. He spoke, and they were healed -- snatched from the door of death. Let them praise the LORD for his great love and for all his wonderful deeds to them. Let them offer sacrifices of thanksgiving and sing joyfully about his glorious acts."

6

Hidden From the Shadow

"No!" Christi put her foot down. "Absolutely not. It just isn't right." Her voice was firm and resolute.

Her boyfriend, David, rolled his eyes. "Please, give me a break!" he exclaimed, exasperated. "You sound like a 90-year-old grandma. It just isn't right," he mimicked her sarcastically. "What isn't right about it? Why do you have such a problem with showing a little love?"

Christi stood her ground. "You already know that I believe sex should be saved for marriage. It's just not something you play around with beforehand." Christi could feel a knot tightening in her stomach. Rubbing her sweaty palms on the couch nervously, she faced David's demanding gaze. This wasn't the first time they had been through this – but it certainly was turning into the most volatile.

"What can God possibly have against two people showing their love for each other!?" David was almost shouting. "Everything I've learned says that God is all about love."

Both David and Christi were attending the same Bible college. "David..." she was struggling to find the right words. "God says in the Bible to stay sexually pure before marriage, and I am going to do what He says. *Bottom line!*"

David stood up angrily and glared, "Christi, if you really loved me you would prove it to me."

Stories from the Living Room

"I said NO!" Christi jumped up and stood toe to toe with her angry boyfriend. "And if *you* really loved *me* then you would stop pushing me."

"All right, this is it!" David threw up his hands. "We are over, Christi." He turned to go, fuming. "I'm breaking up with you. For good." He spit the last words over his shoulder as he stomped out of the room, and out of her life.

Christi watched him go silently, then dropped limply back onto the couch. She let out a sigh trying to expel the pressure she could feel stretching her insides taut. She closed her eyes wearily. "Well, God, I guess it's over now." Yep. It was over. She had obeyed God – and her boyfriend broke up with her. "Lord, please help me to deal with this in the right way."

Christi was sad, but she knew what the Bible said and she knew that because God made her He knew best how she should live. If David only wanted to have her as his girlfriend to have sex, then he wasn't worth the trouble. It was better to have no boyfriend than one like that. Either way, she wanted to obey God, and she knew that no matter how hard and lonely it would be it was the smart way to live. She wanted to live smart.

Little did Christi know how important this lesson was -- that someday her very life would hang on the balance of her willingness to obey.

Christi was not raised in a Christian home. But when she was a little girl, about five years old, a neighbor began taking she and her sisters to Sunday school. Christi loved it. She just loved hearing the stories, reading the Bible and learning about God. She was so loved and cared for by the Sunday school teachers and youth leaders. At the age of 11, she accepted Jesus Christ into her heart as her Savior from sin. How the angels rejoiced that day as a little girl reached out to heaven with simple, childlike faith! Throughout the years Christi continued to go to church steadily, developing strong convictions and a deep trust in God. Inside she had a deep, sure understanding that God was her Creator. She tried to obey Him, because she knew inside that His commands were right. After all, since He made her, He also knew the best way for her to live. It was definitely not always fun, but it was right.

After her college experience with David, Christi didn't really do any more dating, but that fact did not bother her. She enjoyed participating in group activities, and she had lots of friends – both men and women.

Then in the early 1980's she met Greg. She was in her late twenties, and a while after meeting him she went to work at the Foursquare Church. Her pastor there was named Ken, and Greg was his brother. Greg had an amazing testimony - an ex-homosexual and heavy drug abuser from Hollywood, delivered by God. Greg and Christi's relationship slowly blossomed from friendship into love, and they became engaged to be married.

During this time, they governed their relationship with the same convictions Christi had always adhered to. She and Greg both knew that sex was to be saved for marriage, and even though it was not easy, they saved themselves and eagerly awaited the happy day.

Then the constant disagreements and misunderstandings started. It got so bad that they had to postpone the wedding date. Neither one could understand why they were suddenly having these terrible arguments.

"Why is this happening, Lord?" Christi cried out desperately. She hated fighting. "I love Greg – and I know that he loves me." She rested her elbows on her desk at work and buried her face in her hands. "Why can't we just get along?" Their arguments had begun suddenly, but they continued to escalate to the point that Greg and Christi had finally called off their whole engagement and wedding. Yet they both still loved each other – and they knew it. " *WHY*, God?"

Stories from the Living Room

An ominous shadow fell over her desk, blotting out the cold January sunshine. "Christi, come to my office, please." She looked up into her pastor's face, startled by his strained voice.

"Ken, is everything OK?" she asked, alarmed. He just turned and headed towards his office. Christi pushed out her chair hastily and followed. Ken was staring at his desktop when she entered. He motioned for her to sit.

"I don't know how to break this to you," he said, still not meeting her gaze. Christi waited silently. She could see turmoil churning beneath his expression. "It's about Greg." Her face whitened. "He is in the hospital." Ken finally looked straight into her eyes. "Greg has just been diagnosed with Acquired Immune Deficiency Syndrome. He's not just HIV positive - he has full-blown AIDS."

Christi could feel a sickening thud inside her soul as the shock of those words hit her. Greg had AIDS. The next several minutes passed in slow motion – a numb, chaotic swirl. She knew inside that she still loved him. Rising and walking out in a daze, she sat down mechanically at her desk, then got up again and went back to her pastor's office. "Ken," her voice was hoarse with unshed tears, *"what should I do?"*

"Just follow your heart," Ken said quietly.

Follow my heart! Christi's thoughts were exploding in her mind. *I'm terrified, but I do love him.*

Christi went to the hospital to see Greg. He would not let her touch him. They didn't know much of anything about the various ways you could get AIDS and he was afraid she would get the deadly disease from touching his pneumonia, sweat-covered body. They talked at length with his doctor about the disease, and he told them it could basically only be contracted through a transfer of body fluids. The virus is not airborne and you have to get a large dose of fluids into your bloodstream to transfer it.

It's not easy to get AIDS unless you are engaged in an activity that involves a large exchange of bodily fluids such as a blood transfusion, saliva fluids (through dental procedures or possibly "French kissing") and sexual intercourse. If you did those things you were sure to become HIV positive and develop AIDS and then die.

Christi was safe. It felt like a lead weight was lifting off her chest as she thought of how God had protected her. She was going to live. Greg continued to fear for her, but after long discussions with the doctor he was assured she would be okay. Christi was now in awe at what God had done to stop their marriage and literally save her life. She decided then and there to stop asking "why?" when she didn't get what she was so sure was so good and right for her.

Greg lived for another 11 months. Christi could feel her soul bleeding inside as she watched his pain as he wasted away. With his immune system destroyed by AIDS, he was racked mercilessly by viruses and illnesses. He was in the hospital with pneumonia when she first went to him – and he lived through it. His body weathered that battle, an amazing feat for an AIDS patient, but he was doomed to weaken.

For the next 10 months, Greg was in and out of the hospital with three opportunistic infections that most people could resist, but not a person with AIDS. He contracted a salmonella infection, then meningitis, and then pneumonia again. When he had meningitis he had to undergo painful treatments three times a week. The medication for the pain made him freezing cold for hours. As a result of the AIDS his teeth and his hair began to fall out. It wreaked havoc with his nervous system, causing him to do all kinds of irrational things. Christi would rub his legs for hours as his nerves went haywire and he felt terrible burning sensations in his legs. When he was at home, she stopped by every day before and after work to check on him. She took him to the hospital each time he came down with a different life-threatening infection.

In December, 11 months after he was diagnosed with AIDS and just a few days after his 39th birthday, Christi took Greg to the hospital for the last time. He had been in for a routine checkup, and the doctor thought something was wrong, but couldn't put his finger on it. They wanted Greg to stay in the hospital for a few days. He never came home. He had contracted pneumonia again. To have survived his first bout was a miracle – four major infections later, his body couldn't take any more.

The doctor didn't want to tell Christi and Greg's family that it was over. "Look," Christi said sadly, "most of his family lives out of state. They will want to see him before he dies." She knew it was over, and the doctor finally admitted Greg had only a few days to live.

After Christi said her final goodbyes to Greg, she sat alone in the hospital waiting room. Just she and God. All that mattered now was that Greg had a relationship with Jesus. Greg trusted Jesus as his personal Savior and redeemer of his sins. Nothing else mattered. Nothing else could take Greg into heaven after this journey of pain. "His sports car doesn't matter. His friends don't matter," she murmured softly to herself, staring at the ugly, government-green room. "Not even my love for him matters now." That moment would be printed on Christi's memory forever; the green walls, ugly tile floor and the ugly green furniture that matched it. "The only thing that matters now is that Greg knows You, Lord."

Greg's family arrived and said their final goodbyes and the doctors gave him the morphine he needed to ease his pain. Greg died on December 16th. Christi went into a deep depression – she was emotionally exhausted after a whole year of watching Greg fight for his life, of living in the knowledge that he was doomed to die, of watching this disease claim the man she loved.

And there was the confusion she felt ... why did God allow her to love Greg when He knew he was going to die soon? Was it wrong of her to commit herself like that? Was it a stupid thing to do? How could that be God's will? What was the purpose behind all the pain – or was there even a reason for it all?

Slowly and gently, God poured His healing over her spirit. One day as Christi was sharing her thoughts and doubts, one of her friends, Marni, said something she never forgot, "It is never wrong to love someone."

It is never wrong to love someone. God began to show Christi what her part had been in His plan. He spoke to her spirit. *"Your love was never a feel-good, make-me-happy-now kind of love, Christi. It was sheer, raw commitment. You were committed to Greg until the day he died. It was not a stupid thing – it was a God thing."*

"I wanted Greg to have someone who loved him in those last, painful months. Not just a family member... I wanted someone to love him who didn't have to. That's the way I love you. I knew I could trust you to obey Me, Christi."

"I knew I could trust you to not have sex with him, because you weren't married. I hid you from the shadow of death. You could have died of AIDS if you had disobeyed. But you had passed the test before.... I knew I could trust you. Thank you for obeying Me, Christi. Only eternity can tell of the magnificent harvest that shall be reaped from the seed of your obedience."

The fear of God is a mighty and powerful thing. It was that fear – that understanding of God's love for her and the fact that since He made her He knows what is the best way to live -- that kept her alive. Christi is grateful for life and today she is happily married and lives in Cody, Wyoming.

7

A Wagon Tale

I locked myself inside the bathroom like Mommy told me to. Her hysterical screams pulsated through the door, "Lester, you sick pervert; Jenny is only ten years old! Get out of my house before I castrate you!"

I sat on the icy, granite floor and cupped my hands over my ears. Now the only sound was the chattering of my teeth. I drew my knees up next to my uncontrollably shaking body and rocked to and fro while I waited for Mommy to come and get me.

It seemed like forever. My naked rump and my bare feet were getting colder and colder, tingly and numb. I wondered if Mommy and Lester were still fighting. I thought I felt the front door slam. Did Lester leave? Did Mommy leave? I wanted to go look, but my body was stuck in a frozen, bluish knot.

The rap on the door startled me. "Jenny, come on; it's way past your bedtime," yelled Mom.

"M-My l-legs w-won't m-move," I shivered.

Finally, when I was able to crawl over to the door and let myself out, I held my breath while my eyes strained to see through the darkness. By the red glowing numbers on Mommy's alarm clock, I could see she was in her bed, but Lester was not. I picked my nightie up from where Lester had tossed it and slipped it over my head. When I climbed in next to Mommy, she woke up and yawned. "What are you doing? You're freezing cold! Go sleep in your own bed. I don't want to share mine tonight."

"Mommy, I hurt," I whimpered.

"I'll bet you do. You're going to hurt a lot more, too. We really needed Lester's money and now that's gone. Go to bed."

I crawled into my own bed, too bewildered to cry. This was my fault. I wondered all along if it was. The first time Lester abused me I thought I must have deserved it, and every time after that, when he'd molest me or rape me, I guessed I was asking for it, somehow. Now look what I'd done. He was gone. Mommy was angry. We were poor. It was my fault.

In less than a year since Daddy died, everything had become so uncertain, strange and confusing. Mommy got lonely and left my brother and me with different sitters while she went to Parents Without Partners. That's where she met Lester. Later, another man offered her a trip to Europe and she accepted and left us in Lester's charge.

Lester was rich, generous and extravagant and Mommy had a real taste for the finer things. She didn't love Lester but she sure loved his money. She taught piano lessons and made a good living at that, but not good enough to satisfy all her cravings. Consequently, parades of strange men began filing through our lives.

We constantly had to adjust our home and ourselves to Mommy's new boyfriends. Sometimes I felt like I didn't know who I was. "Act nice," she would say. Somewhere between my pretend smiles and my suspicions, I lost who was the act and who was the real me. Some of her men were just one-nighters, but some stayed on a little longer and even tried to befriend me. I never trusted them though. I had never really gotten over what Lester did to me. I didn't ever know what I'd done to provoke him, and I didn't want to unknowingly do it again.

A Wagon Tale

Mommy never mentioned the night she caught Lester raping me. I decided she blamed me for it and hated me too much to discuss it. I was so sorry, though I never told her. I could never find the right time to bring it up. There was such a seal of silence around the whole subject I hated to disturb it.

My brother never knew and Mommy and I pretended like nothing ever happened. Except for Lester's sudden absence and the strict, new rule that nobody except Mommy or me was allowed to enter my bedroom, nothing on the outside looked any different. One night, one of her boyfriends got really annoyed at me and chased me down the hall. When I hit my room, I jumped from my doorway and sailed all the way to my bed without touching the floor. Her angry suitor had to wait outside in the hall. I giggled. He didn't. If he could have gotten his hands on me, he would have whipped me. But I was sure to remind him he was not allowed in my room.

I never told a soul about Lester. Every time a memory knocked, I'd make myself think about something else. Every time I woke up crying from a nightmare, I'd wipe my tears, get up and get busy. I would detonate some loud, pounding music and sing at the top of my lungs or I'd pound on the piano, anything to drown out the demons in my head. I had gotten so good at hiding and camouflaging, that I didn't tell anyone when the next man began raping me, either. I was fifteen that time, and I certainly didn't tell Mom. I had ample blame, pain and shame. I didn't need her accusing looks driving another stake of disappointment into my heart. I finally threatened the creep, and he left me alone.

The damage was taking its toll. I couldn't shake the feeling that it was all my fault. I was doing something bad; I was bad. I withdrew into a world of solitude. I could disappear at will -- at home, or in any crowd, simply with my mind. I trusted no one, liked no one and wanted no one.

I went to a church camp during the time of the second abuse, just to get away for a week. Some of the kids there tried to befriend me, but I wouldn't let them in. I wouldn't even look at them. It was tough, too; they were awfully pesky. They wouldn't let me sit alone, or eat alone. When I shook my head and walked away from group activities, they came after me. I hated being there. Something strange happened though, one night during a worship service. As I sat slouched in the back row, with my arms crossed and my head down, almost asleep, I felt someone touch me. I jumped, but saw no one. When the youth leader said something about the presence of the Holy Spirit, I pondered the possibility. He gave an alter call, and I felt the urge to go forward, but quickly talked myself out of it. God couldn't want me.

I felt like a big, clumsy wagon had been hitched up to my back and it was my penance to drag it around. It was loaded down with burdens of confusion, shame, secrets and fears. When the wagon would hit a bump and the bundles would get shaken and compacted, there would be room for a little more guilt, a little more misery and I'd add it to the heap. Then I covered it up all nice and neat and tied the ends and corners down with tight, perfect knots, so nothing would fall out or be seen.

I actually became quite fond of my wagon. It came in pretty handy for keeping others at bay. I'd just sidle around and park it between me and whoever was too close.

When I was sixteen, Mom was diagnosed with cancer. I took the blame for that, too. I supposed the cancer grew because I had caused her so much grief, so much sorrow, anger and bitterness. Mom had surgery and when she came home, I took care of her. I became her mom. During that time of caretaking, I felt some relief. Mom was completely dependant on me and as long as I was cooking for her, cleaning her, helping and serving her, I felt more acceptable. There weren't too many loving exchanges between Mom and me, and this was an agreeable substitution.

When Mom got sick the second time, I knew she was going to die. After the first hospital visit, I refused to go back. I couldn't stand seeing her wasting away, hooked up to tubes and buzzing, clicking monitors. I hated the medicine smells mixed with her dying body smells. Finally, in 1984, when the doctors had operated until they couldn't operate anymore, they gave her one month to live. She died exactly 30 days later, having never forgiven me.

One night, shortly after Mom's passing, I was working at McDonald's and broke down crying. I made my way into the restroom and just sobbed. Darlene, a fellow employee, came looking for me and when she found me she hugged and patted me and told me she knew someone who could heal my pain.

She took me to church with her the following Sunday. I was greeted with such warmth and acceptance, it was unnerving, but as I continued to go, I liked it. One Sunday, I felt the same presence I'd felt at church camp, but this time when an alter call was offered, I went forward. I got saved when I was 21, just after Mom died.

The pastor and his family welcomed me right into the family. They loved on me, encouraged me, gave me a Bible and taught me how to understand it. This felt more like how I thought a family should feel than my own family ever did. They even invited me over to their house for Thanksgiving and Christmas. I really felt myself opening up and beginning to love them. And as I did, my wagon load got lighter and less burdensome.

Pastor Jack's little Southern Baptist Church split after just a short time and so did he. His family moved on and I loaded up my wagon and did the same. I never even looked for another church. Nobody could ever replace Pastor Jack and his loving family.

About five years later, I was working at another restaurant, and a friendly little couple started coming in. The man told me he was a pastor and invited me to their church, the Foursquare Church. I had never heard of it and certainly didn't want to waste my time investing in something that wouldn't last. I had tried church, and it failed me.

They didn't give up, though. It got downright embarrassing. On Sundays after their church service was over, they and about a dozen of their friends would come strolling in. "If you won't come to church, Jenny, we'll bring church to you," Pastor Kenny's wife, Connie, said. Then she'd introduce me to every single person in their group. They'd all smile and greet me with either a handshake or a hug.

"Great," I said, rolling my eyes and acting way too busy to talk to them. Every week it was the same. I hate to admit it, but I started looking forward to seeing them. One Sunday they had a potluck meal at their church and didn't show up at the restaurant for lunch. I missed them.

On Christmas Eve, 2000, they invited me to an evening candlelight service and I went. Connie ran up to me and almost hugged the life out of me. "You came! You came!" She introduced me to everyone in the church and invited me to sit next to her and her children. They reminded me so much of Pastor Jack's family, but I hated to get my hopes up. Everyone I'd ever cared about had left me.

Despite my cautious attitude, I couldn't help but fall in love with them, and I began attending the Foursquare Church on a regular basis in the spring of the following year. I noticed the joy all around me and I wanted some. My wagon was much lighter again, but I could tell I was missing out on something. Eventually, I talked to

A Wagon Tale

Connie about it. She gathered a group of ladies together and they prayed for me. I felt lighter still, but could not shake the nagging feelings that I was stained, damaged, different and separate from everybody else. I hadn't yet told anyone about Lester or any of my abuse. I intentionally kept it a secret. I was terrified that if they found out about the disgusting things I'd done and the bad person I was, they would reject me, abandon me or kick me out of church. After all, my own mom couldn't accept me after the incidents, how could I possibly expect anyone else to?

I rambled right along though, settling for my unsettledness. I was much happier than I'd ever been before. I decided this was just my lot in life. I told myself, " I'm just not meant to be joyful. I'm the melancholy type. One person's gift is not necessarily another's. My gift just isn't peace…or joy…or freedom…or…."

A couple of years later, a husband and wife counseling team, Dave and Mary, came to our church. *Healing The Broken Heart* was the name of their seminar. I had to work evenings, so was unable to attend, except for part of one session. It happened to be on sexual abuse. I was there long enough to learn that I wasn't the only woman in our church who had been abused as a child. I suddenly felt connected in a way I never had. My heart cried out for me to stay for the prayer part of the meeting, but I had to bolt. I was feeling a little transparent and a lot exposed. Mary didn't know me from John the Baptist, but when I rose to leave, she said, "Honey, I promise there is healing available to you from Jesus. He wants you to know that." I smiled, nodded and left.

I kicked myself as I climbed into the car. "There's healing available, dummy. Why aren't you in there?" I sped away. The prospect of freedom from my pain and shame gave me some glimmer of hope, though. I never forgot Mary's words. About a year later, the class came and went again. I was angry I couldn't attend. I ached for the healing Mary promised.

Last year, LaDonna, a wonderfully anointed lady from our church offered the same class on Tuesday mornings. I had to work Tuesday mornings. As a fit of bitterness and rage began to take hold of me, I cursed and cried out to God. "God, this is so unfair. Why can't I get to these meetings? I want to be healed! Can't You do something? I need some help!"

The very next day, my manager, a fellow Christian, told me she felt like I needed to attend *The Healing Heart* class and she would cover Tuesday mornings for me, so I could go. My mouth fell open and my eyes bugged out. I shook my head in disbelief and unworthiness. God heard my prayer. He made a way.

When I arrived at the class, all nervous and excited, I found out I needed to purchase materials for the course. Quickly, my enthusiasm wilted. I had no money; I couldn't afford the books. LaDonna must have sensed my dilemma and called me into the hall. "Jenny," she said, "don't worry about the books. Someone bought yours for you."

Tears burned down my cheeks. "Who?" I asked.

"They wish to remain anonymous," she said, hugging me.

I remained tight-lipped and apprehensive for about three weeks, but as I listened to several different versions of my same story from the ladies in the group, I felt more comfortable. Eventually, I wanted to get it out and off my shoulders. I cried as I recounted all the gory details of the abuses and of my mom's virtual abandonment. I was not rejected or thrown out by the loving, compassionate women in the circle. Quite the contrary, many arms held me, many words comforted me and many prayers were prayed for me.

At first, I was somewhat embarrassed that everyone knew my deepest, darkest secrets. Shame tried to

A Wagon Tale

overshadow the Lord's goodness. I told LaDonna about it, and the ladies prayed about that, too. One by one, I brought every dark secret into the light, and little by little, the Lord touched and healed each wound. I learned to trust, at first just my classmates, but now those borders are broadening. As I trust God, I can trust anyone He puts in my path, because He watches over me and protects me, and I don't have to be afraid of anyone.

When I first began to trust Jesus, I let Him help me pull my wagon. When I trusted Him a little more, I let Him help me unload my wagon, a burden at a time. Then, I learned the most wonderful thing; He didn't want me attached to the wagon at all! He wanted to unhitch me from the bondage of my past that held me captive in my present. This Scripture in Matthew 11:28-30 really liberated me: "Come to me, all you who labor and are heavy laden, and I will give you rest. Take my yoke upon you and learn from me, for I am gentle and lowly in heart, and you will find rest for your souls. For my yoke is easy and my burden is light."

I don't have that awful wagon dragging along behind me anymore. Jesus set me free! He swapped my burdens for a relationship with Him. When I was saved I felt hopeful and loved, and there is so much more! If you are held down by your past, get a hold of Jesus. Call out to Him. Get to a Christian church. Contact that Christian friend who's always bugging you. Surrender to the One who loves you and has been waiting for you all your life.

8

Little Miracles

Time for Baby! Michelle had marked her due date in bright magic markers on the calendar. It was getting close – February was winding down and their baby was due in March. She was getting excited! Everyone is so nice in the law office where she had been working -- she would miss being here. Today was her last day and in between paperwork she fidgeted in her chair, trying to get comfortable; it was getting harder and harder to sit still for hours every day. Michelle smiled happily as the day drew near its end. Michelle and Jesse had always understood that she would be a stay-at-home mom when the babies came, and she was eager to begin this new chapter of life. There was, however, the nagging worry of money. Her forehead creased for a moment as her mind wandered in that direction. *Would they have enough money in the bank to get by?*

Jesse could feel his muscles tensing as he stared at his paycheck lying limply on the table. Not enough money. He reluctantly raised his eyes to his wife's face. They were two hundred dollars short. Again. "Honey..." his voice trailed off. He looked at Michelle feeling so inadequate. "I don't know how we're going to make it." Minimum wage at Wal-Mart just wasn't cutting it. He swallowed hard, running his hand through his hair. Just their basic expenses totaled two hundred dollars a month *more* than he was making.

Stories from the Living Room

Michelle lowered herself carefully into the kitchen chair and sighed, resting her head in her hands. It wasn't that they spent a lot of money, because they didn't. Both Jesse and Michelle had always tried hard to be good stewards of the money God gave them. "Well, honey," she said quietly, "we know we are doing what God wants us to do, and He will provide a way for us to do it." Jesse nodded. They both knew it was God's plan for Michelle to stay at home to raise their children when the time came, and now that time had come.

He scooped up Michelle's hand. "Let's pray. I need to talk to God about my worries."

The next day Michelle and her friend worked hard getting the curtains made for the nursery. The tiny room was going to be perfect for their new family member. She carefully laid them aside to hang later and began clearing the fabric scraps and patterns off the kitchen table. It was so nice to be home during the day, instead of trying to find a comfortable position in her office chair. Michelle smiled contentedly as she glanced around her kitchen; it was such a darling little house! It was small, but she and Jesse loved it. The lady they rented it from was so sweet, *speaking of the rent...* Michelle's thoughts veered back to their finances. She knew the rent payment was due soon. She had made the mental calculations, but found herself making them again as she opened cupboard doors, assembling ingredients. Fifty dollars short. No matter how she looked at it, they were still fifty dollars short on the payment. Same old answer. Not enough.

"No!" Michelle set a saucepan down on the stove firmly. "I am not going to worry about this. You know our needs, Lord," she looked upwards, "and I know I can trust You to meet them."

The traffic light turned red. "God, help us," Jesse prayed silently as he slowed to a stop and closed his eyes wearily for a moment. Snowflakes began to splatter on the windshield. "I could really use some money, Lord," he said loudly as he looked up. *Swipe, swish, swipe, swish.* The windshield wipers swept methodically across his vision. "Now would be a good time." The light turned green and he stepped on the gas. "I guess things are a little tighter than we expected since Michelle quit her job." It was true. In the excitement of finding out they were pregnant with their first baby, they hadn't realized until later how hard it could be to live on one income. Jesse turned a sharp corner onto the quiet residential street. *Swipe, swish, swipe, swish.* The wipers started working overtime as the snow pelted down. "God, I know we are doing what You want us to do," he braked at the intersection, "and the Bible says You will make a way for us to do what You want us to do. So…." he pulled out into the traffic, "we really need some money." Were the words going any farther than the ceiling of the car? Jesse sighed and pulled up next to the curb. He could feel the desperation tightening in his stomach. He turned the key in the ignition and shut off the car. Opening the door, he strode swiftly across the wet grass, head bowed against the blowing snow. "Hi, honey!" he called out, seeing Michelle smiling in the doorway of their little house.

She waved and held open the door as Jesse hurried up the steps and inside. "How was your day?" Michelle helped him out of his wet coat. "Supper is ready."

"Smells great!" Jesse slipped off his muddy shoes, sniffing the tempting aroma wafting out of the kitchen. "I can hardly wait."

Michelle led him into the kitchen and he sat down. A heavenly, steaming concoction simmered on the stove. She was ladling some onto his plate when the doorbell rang. "I'll get it," Jesse pushed his chair out and went to the door. He opened it and smiled with surprise. "Well, hello, Kenny," he pulled their local pastor in out of the wind and snow. "This is a pleasant surprise!"

Stories from the Living Room

"Hi, Jesse," Kenny's broad grin seemed to light up the hallway. He sniffed the scents of supper. "Smells terrific in here," he said enthusiastically. Jesse started to invite him to join them for the meal. "Oh no, I can't stay," Kenny said hurriedly. "I just wanted to drop by because I have something for you."

"Hello, Kenny," Michelle exclaimed, coming in to stand beside her husband. "It's great to see you!"

"Likewise," he said as he took a plain envelope from his pocket. "Someone from church gave me this for you guys," he said mysteriously, the corners of his mouth turning up in a smile. He handed Jesse the envelope.

"What's this? Who is this from..." Jesse puzzled as he slit open the top with his fingers, and Michelle peered over his shoulder curiously. He reached inside and pulled out fifty dollars.

"Praise God!" he said quietly. "Thanks, Kenny." He looked up at the pastor who was still beaming.

Kenny wouldn't say who the gift was from. "I guess God just wanted to give you some money," Kenny said, smiling and turning towards the door. "I have to go...you two have a great night." He hurried out to his car as Jesse and Michelle watched him go.

They looked at the money in their hands; fifty dollars, it looked like a million. *Thank you, Lord!* They felt like dancing in the hallway with snow blowing in the front door. God came through. The rent was paid on time, just like it had always been.

On March 7th the big day came. Zachary Fowler arrived, welcomed by two of the happiest people on the planet that day. What a wonderful blessing it was, and all of the bills got paid! The money was there when they needed it; they always had enough. One day they received three hundred dollars from a church they had gone to before moving to Wyoming. Another time they came home and found groceries left at their door when they didn't have the money to buy any.

Jesse and Michelle felt so humbled that people would give to them that way. They felt so loved. It was incredible to experience how much God really cared for them, and how much their friends cared, too. It was God coming through for them every time.

Jesse couldn't say where all the money came from, but they always had enough. Jesse and Michelle will be the first ones to tell you that it's not over yet. God is still writing their story, working in their lives. He is still doing His little miracles every day.

God has physically healed my thyroid, sustained me through marital trials, including separation and alcoholism, and is continuing to heal my marriage. He also has continually given me the wisdom and strength to homeschool my kids for 14 ½ years. He keeps me from falling away from Him in the midst of life's trials. I'm so deeply, deeply grateful to Him for caring about every detail of my life. He gives me the strength to go on and to enjoy life. He is so good to me.

9

The Love of My Father

"Daddy, stop it! Don't touch me there!"

My dad's whiskey breath was hot and rapid. "How old are you now, LaDonna?"

"Ten," I whimpered.

"You've become quite a little woman, haven't you?" he whispered. His face was twisted and perspiring and his eyes were hungry as he picked me up and galloped down the basement steps. He pinned me to the cold cement floor with one hand while he unfastened his clanging metal belt buckle with the other. He stripped off my pants and panties -- then he stripped away my innocence. I covered my face and screamed and screamed while he raped me. No one heard. Dad had sent Mom to the store for beer and locked my twin siblings, Kelli and Kyle, outside.

That was the first time my dad raped me, but it was not the last. He had always been very physically and verbally abusive to our whole family, but when my little brother, Kyle, was diagnosed with leukemia, Dads' rage fanned to blistering new heights. After he heard the news about Kyle, he beat Mom so badly she couldn't get up. She lay on the floor most of that night in a broken heap and cried. The next several days her eyes were blackish-purple and so swollen she had to tip her head back and lift her eyelids with her fingers to see. We stopped going to church.

Stories from the Living Room

I wanted to die. I wanted to run away, but I feared for my little sister's safety. I vowed I would do everything in my power to protect Kelli from Dad. That was my purpose. I was like her mama bear, I even slept with her. That didn't keep me safe, though. The nights that Mom was at the hospital with Kyle, and Dad wasn't working or out drinking, he'd sneak in, cover my mouth and take me to the basement. It became difficult to distinguish between when he was really raping me and when I was having my nightmares. The nightmares even seeped over into the daytime as flashbacks and hallucinations that were shockingly colorful and vivid, with every sight, sound, smell, pain and terror of the actual act. They were so real it was as if I was being violated even when I wasn't.

Dad said if I told anyone about our secret he'd kill them. I believed him. I wished he would murder me, instead; I was already dead inside. What he was doing to my body was incomprehensible, but what he was doing to my spirit was worse. I thought, "If my dad wants to hurt me so bad, he can't possibly love me and if my own dad can't love me, who can? I must be hideous and unlovable."

Dad decided to move us into a two-story fixer-upper. I hoped moving out of the old, green house with the old memories would somehow be a fresh start, but when I saw how isolated and dreary this house was, my heart sank. When I walked inside the hair stood up on my body and I felt as if I was brushing up against the devil himself. There was something very dark in that house. Doors opened and closed on their own. Toys played with themselves. It was an icy, dilapidated horror with rooms so dark no light could brighten them.

The darkest room was Mom and Dad's bedroom, where the incest continued and grew worse. It happened more frequently, almost nightly, and it became more gruesome and perverted. This monster leering over and attacking me was not my dad, he was my enemy and I loathed him. He started raping me away from home, too, whenever he could get away with it. One time he offered me money. That was the lowest. Of course, he apologized afterward and promised it would never happen again, but that wasn't new.

My brother was dying before our eyes. We had to quarantine the house and consequently, I missed a lot of school; I couldn't be bringing harmful germs into the house. We were showering continually and sterilizing everything with Lysol spray. It's kind of funny looking back at how hard we worked to keep things clean on the outside, while so much filth existed on the inside. We even diligently busied ourselves rebuilding our house while our lives were crumbling apart.

By the time I was in junior high, I was swallowed up in shame; somehow I blamed myself for the abuse. I perceived myself as very different from my peers. Although I had friends, I was always lonely; Dad really kept his thumb on me. Of course, hanging out with friends or dating was out of the question; he didn't want me "slutting around." He monitored all my phone calls, and wouldn't let me go to the store or anywhere without either his permission or him. I brought girlfriends over a time or two, but I hated the way Dad stalked them with his lustful eyes. Also, he had this evil, satisfied smirk that betrayed his thoughts to me. I feared for their safety.

Dad had lectured and threatened us kids forever about drinking and using drugs. But suddenly he was forcing me to drink before he raped me. He never forced me to take drugs, but he did offer them to me. I never accepted them from him but later experimented with LSD, speed and a few other drugs with my friends. Drugs just didn't do it for me. Deep down I knew they couldn't fix my life. I did consider trying to overdose, though.

Stories from the Living Room

I remember one night after Dad had raped me, shadows were hovering above, laughing at me and threatening to suffocate me. I felt completely crazy. I couldn't take it anymore, the demons, the craziness, the incest, nightmares, flashbacks, shame or secrets. I lifted a butcher knife from the kitchen and took it to my bedroom. I held it to my chest and called on the name of the Lord.

"Jesus, I gave my heart to You when I was a little girl. Are You real? If You are real, prove it to me now. If You can't prove Yourself to me, right this minute, I'll assume You don't really exist and I will stab myself. You are my only hope." Immediately, a bright Presence filled the room. I was immersed in serenity mixed with love. A light reflected off the blade pointed at my heart and the knife flew across the room. That was good enough for me!

I knew this was the Lord telling me, "This is not the time. This is not the way." This encounter offered me the glimmer of hope I sought. I remember thinking, *Maybe God can love me. Maybe I am lovable.*

In June of that year, I went into Kyle's room to take him his dinner. He was fast asleep and I couldn't wake him. I finally shook him. No response. He was breathing, so I knew he wasn't dead. "Mom! Mom!" I called. She raced in and we took him to the emergency room. He had slipped into a coma.

He woke for a brief period in the hospital, and called me to his bedside. He couldn't open his eyes, but he pointed up and said, "Look up, LaDonna! The angels are coming to get me now. Please take care of Mommy, Daddy and Kelli."

I sobbed and caressed his soft face, "I will. I promise."

I know my brother is in heaven. He was an extraordinary little boy. Before he went into his coma he told my Mom, "My spirit man isn't sick." We have no

The Love of My Father

idea where he got that information. In the treatment room, he used to lay hands on the other children and pray for them. And when he used to get afraid, he'd pray in tongues.

That following July our family was preparing to head home from a trip we had taken. We had a small cab pickup with a camper shell and since not all of us could ride comfortably in the front, I volunteered to ride in the back. Dad was too drunk to drive so he crawled in back with me; I begged him not to. I saw that gleam in his sweaty eyes. Despite my objections, he smiled at me and latched the camper door. As soon as Mom started the truck, he pressed himself up against me and gave me a big, open-mouthed kiss. He started pawing me and I slapped his hands away. He just laughed. He pulled me down onto my back and ripped my blouse open.

I had stopped fighting Dad. It only prolonged the misery. I always just lay there pretending I was dead. But this time I fought. It dawned on me how really ideal this was. Mom could catch him in the act. He couldn't deny it and I wouldn't have to tell and get anybody killed. He yanked my pants down. As we struggled, the truck rocked and jolted. I yelled, "No-o-o-o-o-o!" at the top of my lungs, and looked up to see Kelli peering through the rear window. Her mouth dropped open and her eyes grew wide with fright.

"Mom!" Kelli screamed, "Dad is hurting LaDonna! Dad is hurting LaDonna!"

Mom slammed on the brakes and squealed over to the side of the road. She squinted back at us, knocked on the glass and screamed, "What is going on back there?"

Dad pushed me away and fastened his pants. "It's not what you think," he sputtered.

Mom flung open the camper hatch. "What are you doing to our daughter? You dirty &!?&?! get out of here!" she shrieked.

I pulled my pants on while Mom and Kelli climbed over the tailgate into the back of the truck.

"LaDonna, are you OK? How long has this been going on?" Mom asked.

"For a very long time," I cried.

With a string of profanity Dad staggered to the front seat and slammed the door. He floored the gas pedal, throwing gravel in every direction and we sped down the highway. Kelli kept screaming. I kept crying. Mom kept trying to comfort us. We came to a small town and Dad pulled over into a Country Kitchen parking lot. "I'm hungry," he shouted. He banged on the camper shell, "Are you coming?"

Dad stomped inside. When the three of us had gained enough composure we went into the women's restroom. We were all crying and sniffling, holding and patting each other. "Mama, I'm so sorry I never told you. Dad said he'd kill you and Kelli and Kyle."

Just then, Dad busted into the ladies' room. "Come on! It's time to go home. Everything is going to be alright."

But it wasn't. Dad didn't go to work for about a week while he raged and paced and held us at gunpoint. We couldn't go anywhere, talk on the phone, or even speak to each other. Finally, Mom looked over at me and winked, "LaDonna, everything will be okay, won't it, and you're not hurt, right? "

I nodded my head, "Yeah. I'm fine. Let's all just forget about it."

Somehow that appeased him. "I agree," he said. "Let's put this far behind us." He motioned for us to get up off the couch. The next day he went back to work.

The moment he walked out the door, Mom called a lady we used to know at church. She took us in and got us hooked up with Crisis Intervention. I was poked and prodded in body, mind and spirit by detectives, counselors and gynecologists, until they gained sufficient evidence to lock Dad up. He went to jail right away and then he served about a year in prison. He got out early for good behavior.

In the meantime, we lived with my maternal grandparents. Mom had to take parenting classes and I had to go to counseling. Nothing really helped though. I was still dirty, ashamed, crazy, hurting and searching. I built thick walls around myself and wouldn't let anyone inside my heart.

I began going to church with my grandparents and even joined a youth group. Then, Dad was released, and Mom started dating him again. I was sick! How could she? She was putting herself, Kelli and I in terrible danger. Before long, she informed us we were going to be a family again.

"No! I won't go!" I protested. "You can't protect me. Let me stay with Grandma and Grandpa. I'm old enough to make my own decisions."

"Your dad has changed. Things will be different this time. You're still in high school, you're still my daughter and you are coming," she said.

So I went. Mom and Dad moved us back into our old house. Dad absolutely refused to let me go to church and made me drop out of youth group. Back came the nightmares, the flashbacks, the craziness. Being around Dad made me jumpy and always on guard. He knew better than to touch me again, and he never did. He knew I would tell. I hated the way he looked at Kelli, though. I hated him kissing her or hugging her. I told him, "If you mess with her, I will find your gun and I will blow your brains out." And I meant it.

It wasn't long before he started drinking heavily and using drugs again. He was angry and mean, abusive and terribly violent with all of us. He was strict and controlling and still refused to let me go anywhere without him.

"You just want to have sex with all the boys in all their backseats," Dad said.

"I'm not like you," I said coldly.

"You're nothing but a whore."

"You made me one."

Eventually, he did allow me to go out on a few dates, chaperoned by my little sister!

Finally, graduation came. Dad showed up drunk and obnoxious. I fantasized all through the ceremony about just disappearing after it was over and never returning home, but I had received a scholarship to a local university and really wanted to take advantage of it. Besides, Mom was pregnant with my baby brother and I was afraid if I were not around to prevent it, Dad would beat her to death or cause her to miscarry. So, I stayed home for a while, worked, and attended college. One night, I caught Dad gazing at Kelli with his fat tongue hanging out and I couldn't take it.

"You disgust me!" I hissed.

"What?" he asked, not even bothering to take his eyes off her.

"If you touch her and live through the bullet I plug into you, I will report you and you will never see the light of day again."

We ended up getting into an awful fight. I walked out the door and didn't look back for a long time. My aunt checked in on Mom and Kelli for me and kept me up to date. I moved in with my grandparents, again. I bailed out of college; I just couldn't concentrate. As it turned out, God worked all this out for good in the end. Grandma introduced me to a wonderful man named Mark who loved the Lord. Mark had something I wanted and I ended up before God, once again, with an ultimatum. "God, if You want me at all, if You can take this dead soul, wounded spirit and crumpled life and patch it all back together, I'm Yours. I will serve You all the days of my life. I'm at a dead end, again. I cannot take this throbbing, empty pain, guilt and shame that shouldn't belong to me. I cannot take the hallucinations, flashbacks, bitterness, hatred and fear. If You can't or won't take me and fix me, please let me die right now."

In that moment, a heavy peace dropped down over me that I can only describe as being wrapped in God's arms of love. It was a different touch than I was used to. It conveyed deep love, purity, total acceptance and hope that there was something more. I wanted it. I sat on the floor and clasped my hands to my heart. I rocked, sobbed and told Jesus my heart and my life were His.

Mark taught me how to stand on God's word. He gave me healing scriptures he called prescriptions. He showed me how to use the words in my Bible to fight Satan and to renew my mind every day. Thus began my journey of healing and my very difficult journey of forgiveness.

The first thing God wanted me to tackle was my anger, hate and unforgiveness toward my dad. It wasn't easy. A lot of garbage stood between where I was and where I needed to be. I learned that God lets us trade the burned-out ashes of our lives for the beauty of His. I gave Him my bitterness. Then, He touched my heart where it was wounded, where that root of bitterness originated and He healed it. He didn't put a bandage over it, He healed it! With no festering wound, no pain or bad memories, there was nothing to be bitter over and my ashes of bitterness became the beauty of contentment. In that same wonderful way, I traded the ashes of my hate for the beauty of His love; my unforgiveness for His forgiveness; my craziness and stress for His peace; my shame and dirtiness for His clean hands and His pure heart.

I'm thankful now, that Mom and Dad got back together. I see where God was at work there, too. If I had remained apart from Dad, he may never have received the seeds I was able to plant in his life, which God watered and turned into a glorious restoration. I started simply by saying, "By the grace of God, I have forgiven you." He would just walk away… but God was working.

About this time I met the love of my life, Will. We dated for a long time. Will surrendered his life to Jesus, too, and eventually we married. Not surprisingly, problems with intimacy erupted. But the Lord was able to handle that too. We had invited Dad to our wedding, but he accused me of being pregnant and wouldn't come. Then one day he showed up on our doorstep. I was hesitant but God was helping me so I invited him in. Dad told me he was sorry and wished he could take it all back, he asked me to forgive him. I couldn't believe it. That was God's doing!

"I have forgiven you, Dad. And, I love you."

"How could you possibly love me?" he asked.

"It's because of Jesus. He's been right here healing every single pain, every bad memory, every bit of unforgiveness, anger and hatred. He wanted me to forgive you and helped me do it. He loves you too, Dad." I hoped my dad would rededicate his life right then, but I guess it wasn't the time. Besides, I was thrilled with just being able to tell him I forgave him.

A few years after Will and I had moved to Wyoming, I became very ill and almost died. While I lay in bed I felt an urgency to write to my dad and tell him more about God's love, grace, forgiveness and healing power. I didn't want to die without having done all I could to try to get my dad to turn his life back to God. Dad had accepted Christ many years ago, but had turned his back on God and His ways. My life was so full of joy and beauty now and I wanted him to have that, too.

After that letter Dad started calling frequently, which was odd since he hated the phone. Once he called and said that if anything ever happened to him, I shouldn't worry, because everything would be okay. I know that was God preparing me for what was about to unfold.

One day out of the blue, Mom called and said Dad was in critical condition and I should try to get there. I flew there as soon as I could, but not before Dad went into cardiac arrest. When I finally reached the hospital and found his room, I opened the door and saw my daddy. There was no trace of hatred. There was not one bad memory, nothing of the past. God had removed it all. All that remained was pure love.

I went over beside his bed and put my face against his. "Don't go, Daddy. If you have to, I understand, but I want you to know that everything is forgiven." I kissed his forehead. I wanted only peace and good and rest for him. I wanted him to go to heaven and be with his loving Father.

After much prayer and consideration, our family made the decision to take Dad off life support. He would have wanted it that way. He breathed his last breath, like a heavy sigh of relief and his countenance came suddenly alive. The glory of God filled that room. We all said goodbye and released him into the Father's hands. I looked toward heaven and said. "Thank you God, for taking my daddy to be with You."

I guess what I want you to know is God does love us. He loves you. He doesn't want any of us afraid and alone, and though He doesn't cause the bad in our lives, He can and does use it for good. If I hadn't been so hurt and so desperate, I may never have looked up and called for help, and I might never have gotten to experience God or His love, peace, joy and plan for my life. I also want you to know that if God could restore *me* to wholeness and sanity, He can help you, too. And, if He could restore my love for my dad, nothing is impossible for God.

Stories from the Living Room

God is for you, not against you. He created you for a close, personal relationship with Him. Why not call upon God right now? He'll show up. He'll fill that God-shaped hole in your heart that nothing else you've tried was able to.

I was always seeking the adventure of sports, parachuting, driving motorcycles, etc., but none of them could satisfy my inner cry for love, freedom and contentment. God led me to salvation and restored my personality so that I know that I am valuable and loved by God! He is bringing up all the divine gifts and talents He has given me.

10

Caught

No one spoke. Uncomfortable, heavy silence enveloped the three of us like a wet sleeping bag. During the long, dreary ride home, I could hear Dad's furious heart drumming a war dance against his chest. I could hear Mom whispering prayers between sniffles and I could hear my summer flushing right down the toilet.

I don't know why I stole the Play Station. I had enough money in my pocket to pay for the thing. My best friend, Joey, kind of dared me to swipe it and the next thing I knew, a squawking buzzer sounded at the door and I was apprehended by a large, looming security guard. Joey hustled out the door and I was escorted into an inner office. A stern, glaring, jaw-clenching store manager started to dial the police, but for some reason, relented at the last second and phoned my parents instead. What a lucky break! Well, I thought it was, until I saw Dad's enraged expression. My parents and I apologized profusely to the panel of store personnel and, finally, we were allowed to leave.

When we got home, we gathered to have a family conference, but Dad was the only one who had anything to say. "What are we going to do with you, Troy?"

I looked at the floor and shrugged my shoulders.

"Don't you have anything to say for yourself?" he asked.

"No, sir."

Stories from the Living Room

"Well, I have something to say. You're grounded. You're grounded for the whole summer!"

Just then, the phone rang. Mom answered it and handed it to Dad. "Hello?" he said. "Yes, this is he. He stole what?!"

That was my cue to exit. I arose, nonchalantly, from my uneasy chair, but Dad's death grip caught my shoulder. His two eyebrows furrowed into one dark stripe, like a bushy ferret arched across his forehead. "Sit down, young man," he blustered.

The stiff wad of cash in my front pocket jammed into my leg when Dad pushed me back onto the chair. Oh, man! I couldn't get caught with that on me. When Dad turned around to pace in the other direction, I tried to shove the money underneath the cushion, but just then, he spun back and growled into the receiver, "I see it right now. I'll call you back." He smashed the phone onto its cradle.

"What you got there, son? A little cash from a robbery?" Dad asked, smugly.

"What?" asked Mom, putting her hand over her gaping mouth.

"Troy and his partner-in-crime, Joey, broke into the baseball field concession stand and robbed it! You are grounded for the whole summer!" he barked.

"You already grounded me for the whole summer," I said.

"Well, then...you're grounded for life! And stay away from Joey!" Dad yelled.

Joey, his folks, my folks and me had to meet with the head honchos at the baseball field. They decided they didn't want to involve the police. They just wanted a confession from Joey and me and a promise we would never do it again. We had to clean up after ballgames all summer, and we had to pay back all the money. We still had most of it so we just handed it back. My parents also

Caught

tacked on a few of their own creative disciplines. I had to mow their church's lawn and water it twice a week until school started. I didn't really mind though, it got me out of the house.

Every single time I ever did anything wrong, I got caught -- every single time. Somehow, though, I always seemed to luck out and catch some break that either saved me from prison or the grave. Mom and Dad said it was God watching over me, keeping me alive and keeping me safe. I thought if it *was* God, He sure could intervene a little sooner and help me just not get caught. One time, I heard my mom ask God to please always protect me and cause me to get caught every time I did anything wrong. He sure answered that prayer.

A couple of weeks dragged by. Mom and Dad's wedding anniversary arrived and they drove to Red Lodge for dinner. My sisters were at the movies. I snuck out. What all-American, sixteen-year-old, unsupervised boy wouldn't?

I went to Joey's, of course. We ended up at our friend, Eric's, to ride his new motorcycle. When it was my turn, I accelerated a little too much around a corner that was sharper than it looked and my tires spun out on some gravel. The next thing I knew, I was skidding between the wooden posts surrounding the curve. I slid over the embankment and sailed about twenty feet through the air. When I hit the dirt, the bike landed on top of me, which saved *it*, but *I* was in excruciating pain. My right leg was shattered in seven places.

Eric dashed home and returned with his dad. I wailed, cursed and writhed in agony, while Joey, Eric and Eric's dad hoisted my broken body into the back of Eric's dad's truck. I screamed all the way to the hospital.

Upon arrival, a nurse gave me a pill and some water in a paper cup. "Here, this will ease the pain," she smiled. I swallowed it, but it didn't help. She and another nurse wrestled me from the wheelchair to a hospital gurney, and tried to measure how tall I was while I lay crunched in a sobbing, throbbing ball of anguish. The pain medication finally began working, and I felt loopy and heavy, and didn't even wince when an anesthesiologist started an IV in my wrist.

Because I couldn't stand and they had no way to weigh me before surgery, they took my height and didn't figure in how skinny I am, and ended up giving me too much anesthesia. I didn't wake up for three days. When I came to, Mom was sitting in a chair, at my side. Her head was bowed, one of her hands was raised, and the other was on my face. I could hear her intense grief as she prayed for me. The overdose could have killed me, but actually ended up saving my hide; my folks were way too concerned about me to punish me.

We had a heart-to-heart, after I got home. Those talks were always tougher than any punishment they ever dished out. It was easier to be mad at them when they would just ground me or something. But I hated seeing the pained love in their eyes and hearing the strain in their tight throats while we discussed my lousy choices and my even lousier future. I didn't know what to do. I wished they would just leave me alone, let me have some fun and some freedom and stop treating me like a little kid.

A couple of months later, I returned to the doctor for a checkup on my leg. He ended up cutting the cast off. My doc and another physician were completely baffled. I was supposed to have worn the cast for at least nine months. I only wore it for two. They said it was a miracle; they had never seen anything like it. I never did tell Mom what they said or even thank her for the miracle I heard her ask God for that night in the hospital.

All of Mom's "God stuff" made me uncomfortable. I had gone to church some, when I was younger, but it was so boring I couldn't stand it. Later, one of my sis-

Caught

ters started going to The Foursquare Church. She loved it. I went with her, sometimes. I actually liked the music, and the people were pretty cool…but the pastor made me nervous. He looked right through my eyes and into my brain. I could feel him shuffling through my thoughts and reading my secrets and fears. Every word he preached was meant for me.

Afterwards, I always felt so convicted. I wouldn't go back for a long time, well, until I'd do something stupid again and decide I wanted to straighten up. I'd return, looking for solutions, for some way out of my maze. I'd just find more guilt, more conviction and more hopelessness. I wasn't like those churchy people. I knew I was a screw-up. I knew right from wrong. Wrong was just easier and more fun, until I got caught.

I pretty much believed in God. I guess I believed in my own idea of God, of some far off, white-haired and bearded old man with a bad temper. I could not understand why He let such bad things happen if He was supposed to be so full of love. I didn't get it. I blamed God for a lot, I blamed Joey for the rest. He was my leader, I was his dutiful follower. Nothing was ever my fault. I was a victim, my parents were harsh and over-reactive and no one understood.

I thought my girlfriend, Ashley, understood me. We dated all through high school. She wound up pregnant and got an abortion. I was so angry. She knew I was dead set against it. I didn't want her killing our baby, but she did it anyway. We broke up right after that.

I got real heavy into weed and then speed after I graduated and moved out of Mom and Dad's. I had to start dealing to afford my own habits. Drugs were not a very lucrative business for me. I couldn't stay out of them and always used up what I needed to sell. I heard a rumor that the DEA was onto me. The day before they would have busted me, I took off for Arizona.

About nine months later, when I figured things had cooled down enough with the feds, I moved back to Cody and in with my parents. I thought I missed Ashley, but we couldn't make it work again. I had lots of girlfriends after her. It seemed like I behaved better if I had a female by my side. I could pretend to be a nice guy for a while but, eventually, I'd do something rotten and ruin things. We'd break up and I'd hook up with a new girl. Mom said I should find a Christian girlfriend and stop running around so much. *Sure, Mom.*

I went on antidepressants for a while. I was willing to try anything, legal or illegal, that promised to help shake the heaviness that followed me around when I was straight. The Zoloft wasn't very compatible with my alcohol, however, and didn't work too well.

When I turned twenty-one I started hanging out at the bars all the time. Booze made me happy, at least at first. Later in the evening, though, I'd usually become angry and belligerent, pick a fight and get kicked out. I was a dumb drinker. I was snorting a lot of crank, which enabled me to drink all night long and never feel drunk. I guess I probably *was* drunk, I just didn't feel it.

One night, somehow, I manipulated Mom's car keys from her. She had a brand spanking new, titanic, pearly-white Crown Victoria that she adored. She must have decided if she treated me like I was trustworthy, it would make me trustworthy. It didn't work that night.

I promised her I would not go to the bar, but after a little 100 mph cruise through the North Fork tunnels, I landed at the Silver Dollar. I just drank a few beers and was sure I had enough speed in me to keep me sober. So, later, when I was whooping and hollering and racing up the Post Office hill, at 75 mph, staring up at the stars, I was surprised to feel the impact of the windshield against my face when I collided like thunder into the steel guardrail. The airbag exploded and threw me back into my seat.

Caught

It's all that saved my life. At that time, I wished it hadn't. I got my first DUI and spent a week in jail.

The only thing worse than my dad's frenzied, pulsating, red face, scowling at me through the visitor's glass was my mom's tear-streaked, disappointed one. Dad yelled and told me when I got out of jail, I was not welcome in their home anymore. Mom's jaw quivered when she told me she forgave me and loved me and that she was still praying for me. "Troy," she begged, "please use this time to evaluate your life. God may not keep bailing you out forever. Stop testing His patience."

Jail sucked. It sucked so bad I stayed out of the bars for quite awhile after that and tried to straighten up. I spent a few more cozy evenings incarcerated for warrant arrests, then, a couple years later, I got another DUI. After the second one, I went back to church to see if God was there. I needed help. I needed something more than what I was finding in the world and in the bars.

God was there. He showed up in the warm, incredible smile of a girl named Melissa. She hooked me and I just flopped like a fish, while she reeled me in. I returned the following Sunday and mustered up the nerve to ask her to dinner. She asked me if I was a Christian. She said she would never date a guy who wasn't one. I accepted Jesus that day.

My motives were selfish and askew. Nevertheless, God took me seriously. He accepted my half-baked confession of sin and my half-hearted submission to him. He moved me right along into a lighter, clearer place, where I could hear His voice and follow His lead. He delivered me, immediately, from drugs, alcohol and my appetites for danger and self-destruction. I got hungry to know God better, so I began to ask Him for more of Himself. He gave me more. I learned all my preconceived notions about Him were very wrong. As I experienced His love and His presence, I fell in love with Him, and it wasn't too long before I had given Him my whole heart and my total devotion.

Melissa and I dated for about a year, and on the happiest day of my life, she married me. On that day when I stood, weeping, in front of our church, before friends and family, and beheld that heart-melting, perfect vision of beauty, that sweet, lovely, smiling, faithful, Christian woman approaching me in her wedding gown, with her hands full of flowers to become my wife and pledge her life to me, I knew how much God loved me. Melissa and I have been married for over a year and everyday she is a reminder to me of God's love.

We try to go to church every Sunday. When we read our Bibles and stay in fellowship with other Christians, we just seem to fare better. We don't butt heads as often and we are more peaceful. Faith comes by hearing the Word of God and since I need all the faith I can get, I soak up all I can. I especially love Jesus' words, the red letters in my Bible. They really speak to me the most personally and powerfully.

I have been a Christian for two years, now. I am a different person. I am one of those churchy people. Joey, Eric and the other guys are freaked out. I still see them, occasionally. I try to talk to them about God and how much better my life is now, but they don't get it. It's just not their time -- yet. I keep praying they will turn around, too, before it's too late. Joey seems to think religion is just another fix for me, like booze was or drugs or sex, but it's not. The connection-addiction I had with my vices was nothing like the relationship I have with my living God. I've heard there's a God-shaped hole in our hearts that nothing fits except Him. We feel empty because we try and cram anything in that hole to fill the void, but only God fits and fills it perfectly. He snaps in like that last piece of the puzzle and makes us whole.

Caught

I've made new friends at church and keep close to them. I don't ever want to lose accountability, slip and fall and end up backsliding. I'm still a baby Christian and don't always recognize when I'm being deceived, sinning and trying to justify it. I need my Christian friends to keep me straight. I know the devil and hell are very real. Satan had his teeth sunk deep into me. I wasn't strong enough to shake him off by myself, but God pried him loose. With God, all things are possible. I am living proof of that!

Jesus is the Son of God. He took the blame for my sins and died for me so that I could live for Him. All I possess to give back to Jesus and repay Him for what He has done for me, is my life. So, my life is His and I will spend it showing people His love and His kindness. I like telling people what He's done for me. I want them to find what I've found...*Who* I've found. God didn't destroy me when that's all I deserved. He didn't let me destroy myself when that's all I aimed for. He's rescued me throughout my whole life and I want to make Him glad He did.

I used to think happy people were just too stupid to see that life sucked. I thought being a Christian would be boring. However, there is nothing more exciting than seeing God Almighty, Creator of Heaven and Earth, at work. His power is never boring. His love is never boring. He has a plan for my life that includes joy when I'm down, peace when I'm stressed or afraid, wisdom when I'm unsure, strength when I'm weak and forgiveness and mercy for each new day...not boring!

You can imagine how happy my parents are. No more worrying, crying and praying all night long. All of Mom's prayers have been answered...except the one she's praying now, for grandchildren!

11

Dead Girl Running

Bitterness and rage engulfed ten-year-old Eva after her parents' divorce. She felt betrayed by her mom and abandoned by her dad. She, her younger sister, Louise, and her baby brother, Trent, were volleyed back and forth from parent to parent every summer, every Christmas and every new school year. By the time Eva was in the fourth grade, she had changed schools nine times. By the time she hit junior high, she was in her fifteenth school.

Eva had stopped trying to make friends. It was exhausting breaking into tightly established cliques. Besides, once she was inside, it was time to move again. Instead, she buried herself in her schoolwork and in books about other miserable kids; older kids who drowned their sorrows in drugs and alcohol, kids who wanted to die, just like Eva. Eva tried drinking, tried smoking pot and tried inhaling cooking spray from a plastic bag. She decided that the only thing left that might quiet her anguished spirit was death.

Eva was in the seventh grade when they moved again. One evening just after they moved, she shook out handfuls of aspirin and gagged them down with milk. As she fell asleep that night, she was relieved that her misery was finally coming to an end. She awoke the next morning, however, vomiting and spinning with a splitting, ringing headache.

Eva proceeded in a slower death march by continuing to drink, smoking dope and isolating herself. She read books about magic and witchcraft, and listened to music that focused on death and pain. She preoccupied herself with demented thoughts, which she turned into dark poetry and short stories.

In the fall of her freshman year, Eva started another new school. She met a fellow transfer student equally as cynical as she and they became quick friends. Sonya wanted to be a witch and soon, Eva did too. They began skipping school and spending the long days at Sonya's dad's house. They drank beer, smoked cigarettes and studied witchcraft books. They made voodoo dolls of enemies and chanted magic spells. Eva felt black inside. Instead of just doing evil things, she felt she had become an evil thing.

This was one step further down Eva's bottomless, pointless, hopeless abyss. Once again she was losing hold of her weak will to live and once again, she tried to die. She wished she had a gun; she didn't. She would have to use pills. She gathered a colorful variety from the medicine cabinet and chugged down her pill cocktail with a beer. "I really just want to be dead," she thought as she drifted off to sleep.

With her head pounding, she slowly came to consciousness the next morning. "Damn it! Damn it! Damn it!" she cursed. "I'm still alive." She rolled over, slammed her clenched fist into her pillow, and sobbed. Finally, she stumbled into the bathroom. While standing at the sink, she looked into the mirror. Staring back at her was someone she hardly recognized – a dim expression, grayish-pale skin and bloodshot eyes. "What are you doing?" she asked her reflection. A persistent gnawing never left her belly. She knew she needed something else, but what? She had tried everything.

The next year presented a new school in a new town, same ol', same ol'. One Sunday evening, Eva's mom pulled their car into the Holiday Inn parking lot.

"What are we doing here?" asked Louise.

Eva's mom responded, "A friend of mine said there is an evangelist speaking here tonight who is really good. I thought it might just do us all some good."

Louise rolled her eyes. Eva was feeling too gloomy to resist, so the three found seats inside. The evangelist spoke on the gifts of the Holy Spirit. Eva sat straight up in her chair when he mentioned the gifts of healing, miracle working and the power to raise people from the dead. "This sounds more powerful than witchcraft," she thought.

When the man of God asked if anyone wanted to receive Jesus and the power of the Holy Spirit, despite her shyness, Eva stood up. Her mom and sister did, too. Several people gathered around and prayed for the three and invited them to a local church.

Eva, her mom, sister and brother began attending church every Sunday. Many loving people flocked around them. Eva began reading a new Bible she had been given. She started praying. Little glimmers of light began brightening her darkness and she felt accepted, even loved. Eva tried to love back, but there was a wall somewhere in her soul. It made her feel distant, different and very frustrated.

One night, Eva was walking home after listening to a sermon on eternal life. She looked out into the vastness of the universe, at the stars twinkling endlessly. She stopped and stared upward. "God, are You there? I really don't want to live forever, okay? In fact, if You could just go ahead and take me now, I'd be so grateful. I'm no good at life. Please just let me die, kill me now. The hole in my soul is just too big, I don't think even You can mend it. Just take me out. No everlasting life for me, that's too long. This life is too long. Hey! Can You hear me?"

The next summer, Eva, Louise and Trent moved to Cody, Wyoming to live with their dad. They never hooked up with a new church, and it took Eva about one minute to backslide all the way back down. She fell comfortably into a wild crowd again and started going to keggers and smoking pot. She tried acid, speed and mushrooms. "Why would they make this stuff illegal?" she giggled. "It's just fun!"

Eva hoped to reestablish her bond with her dad, but she was so ashamed of the turns her life was taking she couldn't even look him in the eye. She partied on the weekends, and during the week she barricaded herself in her bedroom and studied. Her good report cards convinced everyone that Eva was on top of the world. She maintained a high grade point average and managed to graduate in the top ten percent of her class. She dreamed of going to college and becoming successful as a teacher or a writer, but her desperate, aching wounds and self-destructive behavior kept her going backward instead of forward.

One afternoon, Eva and her sister were sitting in the park when a hippie looking man with very long, dark hair and an unshaven face approached them. "Wanna get high?" he asked.

"Sure," they both said. The three laughed and talked while they smoked on Darien's pipe. They went to a party together and Eva got really messed up, ending up in the back of Darien's van. He told her he loved her, but she knew better.

Eva rented a small house right after her 19th birthday. Darien hung out there most of the time; he didn't have a job and was an alcoholic. He drank from his first hung over breath in the morning until he fell unconscious into bed at night. One day he announced he wanted to straighten up and had joined the National Guard. Two weeks later he left town for boot camp.

An old flame returned to town, shortly after Darien left. He swept Eva off her feet and the two got married. The marriage only lasted three months. After the divorce, Darien reappeared. "I couldn't believe you married that freak behind my back. I loved you. I was trying to become a better man for you and the second I left town you married him."

"You never loved me, Darien," Eva responded.

"Yes, I did. You broke my heart. I still do love you," he said.

Guilt coursed through Eva as she silently swore she would never hurt Darien again. He loved her, he actually loved her and she had broken his heart. "Darien, I never had a clue you really loved me. I thought you said that to all the girls. Please, forgive me."

"You'll have to prove you're truly sorry," pouted Darien. He discovered Eva's guilt was an ace of trump in his hand.

Eva worked two jobs to furnish, decorate and pay for her nice, new apartment. Some sense of satisfaction and accomplishment began to comfort her as her little dwelling took shape. Then, Darien started moving his belongings in and before she knew it, she had a roommate. She would come home at the end of each evening, exhausted from her jobs, and angrily find him drunk or even passed out. Soon, Eva began to drink with him. She couldn't tolerate being sober when he was drunk. She couldn't leave him or change him, so she joined him.

One night Darien got arrested for drunk driving and was thrown into jail. "Get me out of here!" he insisted when he called Eva.

"I don't have any money," she said.

"Get it!" he demanded.

Eva's mom posted the bail money and Darien fled

to Billings. Eva left behind everyone and everything she cared about and ran with him. They shacked up with his parents, who lived in a small, old, refurbished school bus.

Darien and his folks introduced Eva to meth. The first time she tried it an icy, tingly wind enraptured Eva. Every cell in her body shuddered and screamed. She leaned back and grabbed onto the sofa cushion. "Wow!" She sat motionless, at first. Suddenly, she jumped up and began talking excitedly. "This is wonderful, Darien! Let's do some more!"

Day after day, the four drank beer, smoked pot and banged crystal meth. Eva loved the speed. It veiled and softened her downward plunge and, finally, she got skinny! But, when the last of Eva's savings and the drugs were gone, they all got on each other's nerves. They blamed one another for their misery in the hot, cramped living quarters and it wasn't long before Darien's dad kicked them out. "Great, Darien, now where are we going to live?" insisted Eva.

The two hitchhiked, with loaded duffle bags, to a park Darien's mom had suggested, outside of Billings. They found a cozy cranny beneath a bridge that sheltered them from a sudden downpour. They were cold and shivering, but glad to be out of the bus. Suddenly, Darien scurried off, down a ravine. He returned with a humongous cardboard box. "Look Eva, home!"

"Oh, yeah, this is swell," she said sarcastically.

"Well, at least we'll be out of the wind," he smiled sheepishly.

Darien's mom found them a couple of weeks later and warned them the news reported an early snowstorm was moving in. She brought them extra blankets and returned later with a fifth of Peppermint Schnapps and a small woodstove to warm their little cardboard abode. Later, as the two enjoyed their buzz, Darien slurred, "Eva, let's go out west. You're 21 now and legal in every state.

I have an aunt and uncle who live in Oregon and would put us up for a while. It's still warm there, and it's mushroom season!"

"Let's go," said Eva as she drifted off to sleep.

Suddenly, Darien was shaking her and screaming, "Wake up, Eva! Wake up! The box is on fire!" The two quickly gathered their stuff and ran down the embankment. They didn't sleep anymore that night, but shivered, huddled together, beneath their sleeping bags and blankets, watching the embers of their charred box blow through the darkness.

The next day, Darien's mom gave them a ride to the train yard in Laurel. The two hopped up into an empty boxcar and hid just inside the wide open door. After the train stopped in Washington, they thumbed rides to and through Seattle and Portland and over to the Oregon Coast. They caught a ride from a quiet, bearded man who managed a resort on Rockaway Beach. As he pulled in front of the office, he offered them a meal and a shower in a dirty room if they would clean the room afterward. They gladly accepted, then headed for the beach.

"What's down there?" Darien asked, pointing, "Let's go check it out." As the couple drew closer, they identified a roughly assembled hut constructed of driftwood. "Some kids must have built it as a fort. It's perfect!" Darien pulled the blue, plastic tarp from his bag and the two of them anchored it to the top of the fort.

Eva sang, "Welcome to the Hotel California," as they stooped over and stepped inside. Exhausted, they unrolled their sleeping bags and crawled right in. Eva loved listening to the waves pounding a few hundred yards away. "This isn't so bad," she thought as they fell asleep.

One morning, about three weeks later, a little poodle slid down the hillside and landed on their roof. His sharp claws split the tarp and he fell through. Darien yelled, "Get out of here, dog! The tarp is ruined! Let's head to my uncle's." They loaded up and hitchhiked to Dallas, Oregon.

They stayed with Darien's relatives for a few months, then both found jobs and were able to rent a cute little house. It didn't stay cute for long. They burned holes in the carpet and kicked and punched holes in the doors and walls. They fought when they were sober. They fought when they were drunk. Darien began going out with friends, but Eva stayed home and got mad. She felt abandoned and lonely. She became depressed and hope-less. She screamed at herself in the mirror, ripped open her skin with her fingernails and banged her head against the wall. Suicidal fantasies filled her thoughts. Strangely, she felt a presence nudge at her soul. "God, are You really there?" she asked.

She remembered how much better she felt during that short time she attended church. She wondered if Darien would consider going to church with her. When she finally asked him, his eyes narrowed and he growled at her and said, "I am Satan," then he laughed. Eva was afraid. She thought about leaving him. How? She was scared to hitchhike alone. She had no car, no driver's license and no money. She had quit her job and had one secret, tarnished quarter to her name.

Desperate again, she began to plot her end. She thought of dissolving rat poison in Kool-Aid. She fin-gered the poison on the shelf at the hardware store. Lost in her plans to escape the loneliness and hopelessness, she picked up the yellow and brown box. The store clerk interrupted her thoughts, "Got a rat problem?"

"Actually, I do, but this box ain't big enough." Eva set the box back on the shelf. She went to a phone booth and called her mom, collect. "Mom, please get me out of here!" Her mom sent her the bus fare. She left Darien and returned to Billings where her mom now lived.

Dead Girl Running

Eva took a few steps forward and felt inspired. She took an accounting class and went to work for an eye doctor. She got an apartment and pulled herself back together. Then, Darien moved back, with a vengeance. He laid the guilt on so thick Eva relented and welcomed him back. He moved into her place at once, thrilled that she had such a good job. He quickly renewed old meth connections and it wasn't long before they were both shooting up and spiraling down again. Eva quit going to work and they moved back in with Darien's parents, who had upgraded from the bus to a trailer house.

One sunny August afternoon, Eva's sister, Louise, and her husband, showed up at the door. Eva jerked on a long-sleeved flannel shirt to hide the bruises and purple track marks on her arms. "Sorry about the mess," said Eva, as Louise scanned the room. Beer cans littered the floors and tables. Ashtrays overflowed with butts and Darien was passed out on the couch. Eva stepped outside with her sister and brother-in-law.

Louise hugged her sister. "Eva, please come back to Cody with us, right now. You look awful. Mom told me you did. You deserve so much better," she sobbed.

"But, Darien loves me. I can't..."

"Eva, what I saw in there wasn't love."

As weak and confused as she was from being strung out for so long, Eva still knew what Louise said was true. She felt a surge of excitement and a flutter of hope. "Let me get my purse." She kissed snoring Darien goodbye and said, "Thanks for everything." She never saw him again.

As they were nearing the end of the two-hour drive to Cody, Louise's husband said, "Hey, you know who'll be happy to see Eva?"

"I sure do," said Louise.

"Who?" Eva asked.

"Andrew," chimed her sister. "Every single time we see him he asks and asks about you."

"Really? I always liked Andrew."

As Eva filled out job applications around town, she had hopes of turning her life around again, but it was tougher this time. She felt mopped up and wrung back out, as the meth left her system. She wanted to sober up, too, and let go of the beer, but the beer would not let go of her. She was 23 now, and had been drinking from the time she woke up until she passed out, nearly every day, for the past two years.

One day she ran into Andrew. They partied some, began dating and then, he moved in. Andrew liked his pot. Eva stayed drunk. Andrew was in love with Eva, but she wasn't ready for anything so deep. Emotions were messy and interfered with her partying.

Andrew was arrested for giving his friend a joint. He and Eva broke up when he went to jail. Eva didn't want a man in her life anyway; one by one they would try to fix her. She wasn't ready. The pain of sobriety was too much to bear. She was a person she hated, living a life she hated and she needed it all numbed away.

A couple of years later, she bumped into Andrew at a party at Newton Lake. Wow! He was like a new person. He was even more handsome, and dressed very sharp. His dark, wavy hair was styled just right and his blue eyes sparkled something different, something attractive...self-confidence! He had spent time in rehab after completing his jail term and he wore his counseling well. Eva was in love! They started dating again and one summer night, in 1987, Andrew asked Eva to marry him. "Why do you want to marry me?" she asked him.

"Because I love you, Eva. Today my boss told me I have a real future with his company and, now that I know I can take care of you, I want you to be my wife. What do you say?"

"Well, I say yes, Andrew!" Eva said, not restraining her tears or her joy.

This should be the happily-ever-after part, but both Eva and Andrew brought tons of old baggage into their marriage. Eva did not stop drinking just because Andrew wanted her to. Andrew did not stop smoking pot just because Eva wanted him to. Both were sources of friction to the other, but then came crank, the wonder drug they both could agree upon. Andrew absolutely forbade shooting up. He hated needles. So, they snorted and smoked their speed on their short trip to full-blown addiction.

Eva became very jealous and paranoid. She stopped trusting Andrew. She would spy on him around the house and wouldn't let him have any privacy or go anywhere without her. She imprisoned them both with her suspicions and erratic behavior.

Andrew pulled into their driveway late one night after being out of town and found Eva in the front yard. "What are you doing, honey? Why do you have our lamps all around the yard?"

"I'm pulling weeds. Wanna join me," she giggled. Andrew coaxed her indoors. She was busy all the time. She didn't have time for Andrew. She seldom came to bed, didn't eat and didn't even stop to drink. Alcohol finally fell by the wayside. It hampered her speed high, anyway. She quit her job and didn't need to sleep anymore. Eva cranked all the time.

Andrew made promises to appease her paranoia. He started trying to set boundaries for Eva on her crank usage. "Just this much today, Eva, huh?" he'd say, showing her the lines of meth he'd drawn out for her for the day.

During one of her paranoiac rages, Eva told Andrew she was leaving him. The line between what was real and what she feared had become blurred. He begged her to stay. "No, I can't trust you anymore," she screamed.

"Please, Eva, please stay. Let's stop cranking for a while. It's destroying us. Let's quit and if you still feel the same way, I'll leave."

She was so angry, all she wanted to do was get higher. The last thing she wanted to give up was her comfort, especially when she needed it the most. However, deep down, Eva knew Andrew was right. On August 25, 1997, Andrew quit using crank. On August 26, Eva quit...she had a little stash to use up first.

The first days of sobriety sucked. As the numbing wore off, Eva began to feel. She felt the pain of old, unhealed wounds and at this desperate, empty, comfortless time, Eva called out to God. She sobbed and poured her heart out to Him, asking Him, again, to please help her or kill her or do something to save her from her misery.

Eva spent her days in despair, just sleeping and eating. One day would finally turn into the next and then the next. Soon, Andrew and she had a week under their belts, then two, then months, even years! They never used meth again...and temptation was everywhere!

As Eva's mind became clearer, she began to think about God more and more. She dug out her old Bible and began to read the crumpled, stained pages. "God, are You still there?" she asked. She was sure she felt something, or someone.

Eva's mom gave her a workbook called *Experiencing God,* and told her to read it. She took it home and dug right in. As Eva read the pages and filled in the daily questions and assignments, she felt a hunger being satisfied. She began to feel closer to God again. She asked for forgiveness for turning away from Him and asked Him to take her back. Eva rededicated her life to Jesus. In the final chapters of the book, it talked about the importance of fellowship within a church body, and Eva knew God was calling her to find a church. Nervously, she asked

Andrew if they could go sometime.

"Sure," he answered. "After Super Bowl Sunday, we'll go."

When the Sunday arrived, Eva primped and dressed in her favorite flowery dress and Andrew wore his nicest Levis and a silky shirt. When they climbed into the car, Andrew asked Eva where she wanted to go. "I prayed about it," she said. "And a sign I saw, FOURSQUARE LUTHERAN CHURCH, sticks out in my mind. I think we're supposed to go there." She gave Andrew directions, but no such church was there. "Well, maybe it was up on the hill," she said, confused. "Let's go look." The church wasn't there either.

Finally, growing a little frustrated, Andrew said, "When I was a kid, we went to a real nice church near my folks' house. Let's just go there, it's getting late."

"OK," Eva said, bewildered.

When they pulled up to the church, Eva read the sign in the yard: Trinity Lutheran Church. "This will be fine," she thought.

Many smiling, hugging, handshaking people greeted them as they entered and made their way to the back row in the sanctuary. The music was wonderful and Eva and Andrew read the words projected on the front wall and quietly sang along. The pastor talked about nothing being too great for the Lord to forgive. He said, "Come as you are. God loves you and desires a relationship with you. Don't try to get perfect first. You can't. Nobody is perfect. God wants you just the way you are…"

At the end of the service the pastor whose name was Kenny, began praying, "I sense there is at least one person here today who believes they aren't worthy. No one here is worthy. But all we have to do is ask Jesus to forgive us of our sins and be Lord of our lives and He'll wash our unworthiness away. With all eyes closed, is there anyone who wants what Jesus offers? Do you want to begin a new life, born again? If that is you this morning, I want you just to look up and meet my eyes and I'll simply agree with you."

Eva hoped, but never imagined, as she felt Andrew move slightly. Then, she felt his head raise. Pastor Kenny asked, "Are you looking at me?" She felt Andrew nod his head, up and down. Pastor Kenny said, "I agree with you. You are born again." Tears streamed down both their faces as they squeezed each other's hands.

After church Andrew said, "Eva, it was so awesome! I felt God lift my chin! I fought him and pushed it back down, and he lifted it up again! I actually felt him!"

A few days later Eva called her mom and told her all about it, and how curious it still was to her that they'd never found The Foursquare Lutheran Church. Her mom said, "Eva, that church by Andrew's parents *is* the Foursquare Church. They bought it from Trinity Lutheran, about a month ago."

Eva laughed while she cried when she hung up the phone. "God, You did that, didn't You? You brought us exactly where You wanted us to be."

As Eva allowed the Lord access to her body, soul and spirit, He began to heal her. She began to relinquish control, as she leaned more and more on God. As she trusted God, she was able to trust Andrew again, and actually began to let her husband breathe...some. They are learning to honor and love, unconditionally, each other and God.

They are so grateful to their Lord for delivering them from the bondages they were encapsulated in. He saved and healed their deteriorating lives and marriage. He set them free from drugs, alcohol, cigarettes, jealousy, fear, suicide, control, depression, pornography, darkness, demons, death and doom. God restored Eva's close relationship with her dad while he taught her to drive, when she was 38 years old! God has exchanged Eva's sorrows for joy.

At first Eva was confused about worshipping God. She wondered if it wasn't a little prideful of God to insist that they praise Him. But now that Eva has come to know God and has experienced His amazing grace, salvation, deliverance and healing, she *wants* to worship Him. She loves to worship Him. She is thrilled now that eternity is part of her future so she can thank God forever for intervening throughout her whole life -- keeping her alive and safe, and for all He has done and all He is.

I have always known God and the stories of the Bible. My grandparents and parents are Christians and it has carried over into my adult life, and now to my own children. I am 36 years old and can look back and see God in every step I've taken -- even when I didn't know it. I thank God for my grandparents making a stand for God, and the blessings of that have passed down to four generations now. Thank You, Lord!

12

A Good Father

I raised my hands to the sky and cried out, "God, why can't I have a baby? I would be such a good mommy. I have this hollow, gnawing, throbbing cavern in my soul that only a child can fill. I thought this time the adoption would go through. My heart is breaking. What about the promise You gave to Richard?"

I sobbed and sobbed as utter hopelessness replaced my last trace of hope. I was 51 years old and some of the time I felt too old to begin a new career as a mom, but most of the time I looked forward with excitement to God fulfilling his promises to my husband that he would have a son and would name him Samuel.

Because of medical reasons we couldn't have a baby on our own. We were sure adoption was the answer. Well, that's much easier said than done! Adoption is very expensive. Richard and I married when he was 40 and I was 42 -- our age was a strike against us. We didn't have the $10,000-$15,000 minimum it would take to adopt a baby -- strike two. I am an insulin-dependent, Type I diabetic -- strike three. Looks like we need a miracle. So, with great faith, we prayed for that miracle. And we prayed and we prayed and we prayed. "Huh," I thought. "A lot of good that did!"

In the beginning, we followed up on every lead we heard about, and we heard about a lot of them. After a while, we wondered if we were getting in God's way and we backed off to give him room to work. We stopped chasing leads and instead prayed and hoped that maybe this time it would result in a baby for us...nope, well, maybe this time...maybe.... After years of frustration, I got mad and gave up.

That's when I decided it was time to get rid of all my accumulated baby things. I took my nursery decorations and put them up in the Nursery at the church. I gave away several things and put away others. I had a special quilt my grandmother had made for me before she died in 1964 that I had kept all these years. I decided to give it to my niece as soon as she got pregnant.

I held the soft flannel quilt to my face and cried. "Oh, God, why would You instill such hope in our hearts, just to yank it out? Did we misunderstand You? Why, God Almighty, are You so powerless on my behalf? Why do so many others have babies and not us? People who don't even want families have scads of children, and we can't have one? Help me understand."

My memories ushered me back a few years, to the spring of 1996, when I had driven from Cody to Colorado Springs to spend a week with my good friend and my cousin. I was really looking forward to seeing Lois and Kathy. They were encouraging and fun and I needed both things. As I drove, I began praying and told God how very tired I was of fighting about the whole baby thing. I needed to be refreshed. I was exhausted.

God answered that prayer. The room I stayed in at Lois's had a book sitting by the bed. I picked it up and glanced through it. I read parts of it. Through that book God changed my focus. I began to see very clearly that Satan has a plan to destroy all children. He really hates children -- all children, so he tries to destroy them. If he can't get a mother to abort her baby, his next endeavor is to get young women to have babies and keep them in dangerous situations that are bad for children. He will then destroy the child -- physically, emotionally or spiritually.

For so long I had been angry with God because we didn't have a baby; meanwhile, many babies were being born into terrible situations. I now understood I needed to direct my anger and energy into praying against the destruction Satan has planned for this generation being born. I started praying for each and every child I heard about who was still in the womb or newly born. I directed my energy from anger *at* God into prayer *to* God.

In 1999, I met Paula. She and her new husband, Jeff, began attending our church and she and I started praying together once a week. One Friday, Paula asked me to pray for her sister-in-law who was 17 and pregnant. Margie has several physical and emotional problems because she was born with Fetal Alcohol Syndrome to an alcoholic mother. I prayed for Margie and her baby that day and whenever I thought of them.

A few months later, Paula had asked for special prayer. We met at the church on Tuesday, July 18, 2000. I arrived ready to pray for Paula, but she began talking about Margie. She said because of her sister-in-law's physical condition, specifically her heart, the doctors had decided to take the baby. He was born July 12th, six weeks early. They were convinced that Margie could not carry him any longer, and they were sure the baby would be fine. He was tiny, only five pounds, but healthy. Margie loved little Jesse Michael, but her family knew that Margie could in no way care for a baby; she really wasn't even able to take care of herself.

Paula sobbed and expressed her concern over what to do with the baby if they could get Margie to give him up for adoption. I very calmly said, "The most important thing of all is to get this baby into a godly home. If she decides to give him up, give Richard and I a call. We'll take him." I'm amazed at the miracle God had done in my heart. I was not at all excited that I might get a baby.

Stories from the Living Room

I did not try to push for more information. Nothing. Was I so very hopeless? No, not any more. I wasn't hopeless, I was focused. God had changed my focus from myself and my desire to have a child. Now I focused on what was best for that child.

After we prayed, I left for a daylong shopping trip to Billings. When I got home that Tuesday evening, I was very surprised to see Richard's car in our driveway. He had been at our church camp, and was supposed to be in Ten Sleep for almost two weeks. The camp computer was having a serious problem so he made the two-hour drive home to get what he needed to repair it and then go back. I did think about the baby that had been born for a quick minute, but I decided not to tell Richard about him. He didn't really have much time for listening, and sure didn't need to have any unnecessary worries right now. He worked late, went to sleep, got up early and went back to camp. Richard did not know this baby existed.

Three days later, at 6:15 a.m., the phone rang and woke me up. It was Paula. She said, "You asked me to call you if Margie agreed to give the baby up for adoption. Well, I'm calling. She has agreed. He is yours if you want him."

"IF WE WANT HIM?" I said, "YES! DEFINITELY! WE WANT HIM!"

I immediately called the camp to tell Richard he was a daddy. No answer. Circle J Camp in Ten Sleep is in a deep canyon. There is no cellular service there and no one was answering the camp phone that early.

I was in shock so I just kept on moving and doing things. I called our attorney. Richard was an active attorney at that time, but we had also gotten one who would be available to help us in the event of an adoption. He was just getting ready to go for a run. Instead, he got dressed in work clothes and went to his office and began to draw up the necessary papers for the adoption of our son. After this, he was leaving for a three-day fishing trip. I had caught him just in time!

Again, I called camp to tell Richard. No answer. I called Connie Lee, our pastor's wife and good friend. She was thrilled over my astonishingly good news. She had waited and prayed with us every one of these eight long years. We both cried. I was still in shock, buzzing on the inside and numb on the outside. All that day, and for the next few days, Connie was my only link to sanity. She told me what to do, how to do it and when to do it. *Thank you, God, for Connie!*

After talking to Connie, I called camp to tell Richard. No answer. For the next hour or so several calls were made back and forth between the hospital, Paula and our attorney so he could get all the necessary information for the paperwork. Every time I hung up the phone I would immediately pick it back up and call camp to tell Richard. No answer! No answer! No answer!

At 8:15 a.m. the attorney phoned and said that everything was signed and set except for one thing. He said we needed to know about a clause that stated we could change the infant's name. Margie had crossed it out and initialed it. We couldn't change his name. Jesse Michael is a wonderful name, but we had our hearts set on Samuel Richard.

I called camp, again, to tell Richard. The phone rang a few times and *finally* someone answered. I told the camp caretaker's wife who I was and to *please* get Richard. It was extremely important! Finally, he was on the phone.

I took a deep breath and said, "We have a son."

"What?" he asked.

"We have a son."

I have no idea what I said as I recounted the details of how our little family was coming together. I know we both wept and wept. I did tell him that Margie had named him Jesse Michael and didn't want us to change his name. Richard said, "His name is Samuel."

I said, "I know his name. You're the attorney, tell me what to do." Then, suddenly, I remembered friends of ours who wound up in the same situation with their second adopted son. They added to his name. So, our tiny, little baby boy had an impressively longwinded mouthful of a name: Samuel Richard Jesse Michael. Samuel is the name God told Richard to give his son. Richard is the name of Samuel's daddy and grandfather -- both godly men. Jesse Michael is his name from his birth mother who loves him very, very much.

After I hung up the phone from Richard, Paula called and said the baby is ours, but Margie would like to feed him one more time. "Is that OK?" Paula asked.

"Of course," I said. "We've waited eight years, we can wait two more hours to meet our son!" Because he was so tiny, they had a feeding tube in him. He was being fed every two hours. One feeding was from the tube and the next was with a bottle. Margie had to wait until his next bottle-feeding. We all waited.

I called Connie to tell her that we were waiting. "What should I do now?"

"Get dressed!" she said. (She was always full of great advice.) So I did.

By 11:15 I had Connie on the phone again. "I'm on my way to meet my son!!!" She was on her way, too.

I walked into the ward and headed to the Nursery. I told the nurse on duty who I was. She was expecting me. "Wash up, put on a gown and go on in," she said sweetly.

Samuel was in an isolette in the Nursery. My wee baby was hooked up to oxygen, a heart monitor attached to his foot and had a feeding tube. I hated hospitals. I hated the sounds, the smells, the tubes and the wires, all of it. They usually upset me terribly. Not this time though, none of it bothered me. That was a miracle in and of itself!

I entered the still room. My body shivered with excitement. Tears streamed down my cheeks. I put my hands in the hand-holes and began to touch Samuel and I said, "Hi Samuel. I'm your mommy!" Diana took him out of the isolette and handed him to me. All my hearts desires were fulfilled in that moment. I sat down in a rocking chair and just looked at him, cried and talked to him.

The doctor scooted another rocking chair up, knee to knee with me. "This baby is perfect," he said. "He has none of his birth mother's problems. He needs a little bit of oxygen to help him, especially when he eats so he won't have to work so hard to both eat and breathe. Often when a mother is physically stressed like Margie was, the baby is stressed in the womb, and the result is a strong infant. He is very strong."

Richard burned rubber all the way to Cody, and arrived late Friday afternoon. We immediately went up to the hospital to see Samuel. Richard's jaws clenched and his hands trembled while he laughed, cried, talked to and tenderly held our magnificent, yet tiny miracle. We stayed at the hospital most of the day and never missed a bottle-feeding. We were awake early on Saturday and back up to the hospital. Connie had telephoned most of our church family and we received many calls and visits. Everyone was so happy for us, we felt so loved.

Paula called and said that Margie wanted to meet us. Richard and I were terrified. Would she change her mind, right there in front of us? Would she take our baby back? Oh God! I couldn't bear that possibility. I sat down and cried and Connie prayed for me. She prayed that I would remember that Margie was not our enemy. It dawned on me that this was actually the realization of a long-time dream coming true for me. I had dreamt of being able to speak face to face with the birth mother of our child and tell her of our deep respect for her and for her decision and her incredible sacrifice.

We met on Saturday, July 22nd in our church basement. Richard, Connie and I arrived and went downstairs and waited. Soon Paula and her husband, Jeff, were introducing us to his sister, Margie, his brother, John, and their mother. We all gathered around a table. As I began to talk, God filled my mouth. "Margie, we cannot pretend to know how you feel. We have not had to make the sacrifice you are making, but we do understand it is the biggest sacrifice of your life. We appreciate what you are doing and we do not take it lightly. Our baby will grow up and know that you love him deeply and that giving him up was the single hardest thing you ever had to do. He will know that you gave him up because you love him and want the best for him; that you wanted to raise him yourself, but were unable to do so."

The meeting was highly emotional. While Margie spoke, Connie took notes for me so I could record her words later. She said, "My son is precious to me and I love him. He changed my life 100%. I want what's best for my son. My goal is to live for Jesus and become who God wants me to be so my son can respect me when he is older. I want to meet him when he is grown."

Margie brought gifts for the baby: a musical bear, a Noah's ark sleeper, cap and blanket, a tape of kids songs and a letter she wrote to him. She gave us the card of his original footprints, and pictures taken the day of his birth.

We asked Margie if she would mind giving us some history on Samuel's father. With her head down, in hushed agony, she said, "He is of German descent with a little Cherokee. He is 6-foot tall, blue eyes, brown hair. He is 48 years old. He has bouts of manic depression and a temper. He has another son (from a marriage many years ago), and a daughter somewhere. He has no re-morse or love for them. He is not a Christian and wants no involvement in the lives of these children." Then, Margie looked right at Richard and said, "But now my son has a good father."

We all prayed for one another as the meeting came to a close. Margie fell into her mother's arms and sobbed huge, deep sobs. This meeting made it possible for Margie to break from the baby and know he was going to be okay. Now she could begin to rebuild her own life. It was a divine appointment and had divine results!

Since Monday, July 24, 2000, Richard, Samuel and I have been together as a family; a family designed by God. God kept His promise and was faithful, even when I gave up. I have a good Father, too.

> My old life was full of alcohol and I thought it would take care of all my problems, but now with God's great love I understand that that's not what my life needs to be about. With God I have found purpose and meaning in my life. Through all that, God has broken down my walls and softened my heart to love everyone, even people who have hurt me.

13

Growing Pains

White. Sterile. Cool as stone. The hospital walls seemed to close in on Jill as she waited for the doctor to appear with her baby, her tiny, little Jessa Rae. It had been a long, hard road that led up to this moment. For the second time, Jill and her husband, Clay, were at the Mayo Clinic with their baby. Little Jessa was undergoing yet another surgery on her tiny body. Jill was desperately conscious of the fact that baby Jessa was going under the knife in another room. She remembered Jessa looking up at her with a smile before they took her away. Almost like she was saying, "Everything's gonna be okay." Jill felt her eyes smarting with tears as her mind ran over the last several weeks of this nightmare.

It all began right after Jessa was born. Clay and Jill began to notice that there was a lot of blood and mucous in her diapers. About five weeks after her birth the doctors said they thought the newborn had Rota Virus, and they would just have to wait it out. Fine. They could do that. But Jessa's symptoms did not go away – in fact, they worsened with time. She began to lose weight and ceased to thrive like a growing infant should. At the hospital in Cody they ran tests, but could not provide an answer.

"I'm sorry," the doctor said, his forehead creased with concern. "We can't really find anything that could be causing this. You'll have to take her to Billings."

Clay and Jill took her to Billings, hoping to find

the answer. After taking one look at the suffering baby, the doctor there said, "I think she is allergic to your milk. Don't do any more breastfeeding, and I can prescribe a formula that should take care of the problem." *Thank God!* Clay and Jill met each other's glances with enormous relief. While it made Jill sad to no longer feed Jessa herself, she was willing to do anything to find a solution for her baby.

But their daughter's health still did not improve. She just wasn't getting the nutrients she needed. They had to insert a tube into her tiny body near her heart to feed her, which meant surgery. The Lynns stayed over a week in Billings while the doctors ran more tests. The end result was the same as it had been in Cody.

"We are sorry, but you'll have to take her to another clinic. We've done everything we can do – we have basically run out of options."

Clay and Jill thought over the list of recommended hospitals. "The Mayo Clinic has a good reputation," Clay said, his jaw resolute. "We need to go to a doctor who can really figure out what is happening here." Jill agreed. The Mayo Clinic was also close to her family, so they would have a place to stay not far from the clinic.

Jill and Jessa flew to the Mayo Clinic. Clay and their two young boys drove, arriving two days later while older sister, Tashia, remained in Cody to go to school. A specialist at the Mayo Clinic agreed with the diagnosis that Jessa was allergic to her mother's milk, and he prescribed a new formula. It seemed to work – Jessa started to improve. The feeding tube was removed! Clay and Jill stayed over a week to make sure everything was really all right. Jessa was doing great, so they all drove home to Cody.

All too soon, Jessa's symptoms returned. Her tiny body fought to live, but she lost more and more nutrients and became severely dehydrated. Jill shuddered as she remembered their frantic drive to the Billings hospital – they had barely made it in time. She and Clay decided to just bypass the Cody hospital; they knew nothing could be done there. At the Billings hospital they got Jessa rehydrated and stable and then recommended Clay and Jill take her back to the Mayo Clinic right away. *God,* she cried out inside, *why is this happening to us?* Questions pounded in her head as she and baby Jessa boarded the plane for the Mayo Clinic – again. Again, Clay and the boys made the drive, and Tashia had to stay behind.

Now, sitting in the waiting room, those questions came flooding back. Jill could feel fear trying to slip icy talons around her. *Is my baby going to die?* The doubts seemed to hammer her soul, one after another. *Why are You letting this happen, God? I know You can make Jessa well.* She was trying to hold back tears, thinking of her baby in surgery. She'd had tubes and lines put in all over her little body. *God, please just help me,* she pleaded. *Speak to me.* She could feel the stress and weariness building pressure against her brain, like a lake of water behind an earthen dam.

Jill looked up as the door opened. A nurse towered in the doorway. She hurriedly handed Jessa to her mother. Jill stared at her baby, not believing her eyes. The feeding tube stuck out Jessa's neck at a strange angle, and she was still splattered with blood from the incisions. Jill felt an anger boiling up inside her that she had never experienced before.

"I want to talk to the surgeon," she said evenly, gazing daggers at the nurse. "He should have come down to see me himself." Whether it was the look in Jill's eyes or the standard procedure of what to do, the nurse hurried to fetch the surgeon. *God, I'm really angry,* Jill held tightly to her baby, *help me stay together here. I feel like I could blow up in pieces.* The surgeon appeared and Jill stood and confronted him. "This is really sloppy," she said, motioning towards Jessa. "Can you please fix this and get her cleaned up?" She was frustrated with his five o'clock, time-to-go-home attitude, but she stood firm. "This is her life – she can't wait till tomorrow!"

The surgeon agreed and took Jessa out of Jill's arms. When he was gone she slumped back into the chair. *I can't believe the anger I feel inside, Lord. I am not an easily upset person.* Jill knew the stress of having Jessa in the hospital, being away from home and having her life turned upside down was stretching her to the max. *It feels like I am going to snap – like I am being slowly stretched on the rack.* She knew Clay and the boys were under pressure, too. *God, I need peace. I need strength, and I need it NOW.* Jill buried her face in her hands, unable to keep a sudden flood of tears from spilling over.

Slowly she could feel something wrapping around her spirit in folds. Like invisible, warm hugs. Peace. She let her mind drown in it. Let her tense muscles relax. Let her tears flow. *Jill, I will take care of Jessa.* She heard the gentle, powerful voice of God speaking to her soul. *I will take care of everything. I am calling your spirit to grow with me. Calling you higher to a new level.*

"I am ready to let her go, God," Jill whispered, her head still in her hands. "If that is Your will." In her body she was still sitting in a hospital chair, slumped over. In her spirit she knelt before God, ready to surrender her child. She knew God would take care of Jessa. Strength and peace seemed to pour into her, almost like water from a pitcher above her head.

Things didn't change instantly – Jill still had to take each step of the journey – just like Abraham in the Bible, leaving his homeland at God's call. But she had an assurance and a peace that God would work His will. Often, during the waiting times when Jessa was undergoing tests, Jill went down to the playroom and prayed over the kids who were patients at the Clinic. There were so many of them, contending with terrible illnesses in their young lives. It was an unforgettable experience, getting to know these kids and their families.

Clay and Jill were on an emotional roller coaster. They experienced anger, joy and impatience. The waiting was incredibly hard.

Finally, the doctors determined that Jessa had acute chronic colitis, as well as the Rota Virus and a small allergy to protein. They could not totally determine the cause of the colitis, and therefore feared it might be Inflammatory Bowel Disease (IBD). If it were IBD they would most likely have to remove Jessa's colon. For now, they put Jessa on steroids and sent them home. They had to keep her on steroids for some time, and told Clay and Jill that after she was taken off of them it would take a few months for them to see how she would react.

Even through the waiting, God was faithful. Once, Jill begged Him for a sign, something to let her know that Jessa was getting well. She felt ashamed to ask, but she was desperate. Jessa was going through about seven to eight diapers a day, and the day after Jill asked God for a sign Jessa went down to three or four a day. *Thank you, Lord!* Jill felt a new surge of strength rush through her. She could feel her spirit growing through the pain. In spite of the stress and pressure of a seriously ill baby, the Lynn family grew closer together. The growing pains stretched Jill's spirit and she could feel herself drawing closer to God. Trusting in Him in a deeper way than ever before.

Then the big day came – they took Jessa off the medications and waited to see how her little body would react. She did great! *Thank you, Jesus!* They praised God, sharing with others how He had been faithful to save their baby girl. Then came the final trip to the Mayo Clinic. This time the whole family went, Tashia, too. They took Jessa in for her checkup and she received a totally clean bill of health!

14

Reality Bites

Once upon a time there was a young and beautiful princess. She had eyes of a clear and sparkling blue and an uncanny knack of sensing truth from lies in anyone she loved. Never did anyone break their trust with her, for if she saw through their lie they would be banished forever. She lived in a wondrous world where it seemed that everyone loved everyone else. All the people in the kingdom were sure that nothing hurtful or troubled ever disturbed the peace of this kingdom.

One day, as the princess strolled along, partaking of the lovely scents along her flowered path, she met a handsome young man. He had eyes that shimmered and wavered in the clear light of the soul they mirrored. She knew at once that here was a man of honor and dedication in whom she could place her trust forever. That he was a young man without a father or land or deep training in skills did not waver her faith. They fell in love at once and decided to be married as soon as possible.

Her father, the King, said, "Nikki, are you sure you are ready to begin your own kingdom at such a young age? Land I can provide for you, but a kingdom is a heavy burden, which requires constant care. It isn't something to enter into lightly."

The Queen, her mother, said, "Nikki, are you sure you're ready to leave your home and your beloved flowers, your friends and the people who love you at such

135

a young age? Maybe waiting until spring when the green of the grass is fresh and the blooms on the tulips are deep with color would be a better time? Don't you think?"

The wizened counselor, the ever pessimistic toad, said, "Nikki, it is foolish to be married so young. You will end up with a kingdom full of dolts who will drag you down with their ever-increasing demands. You will never be able to move your bed up to a high and pleasant tower."

But the princess and the young man did not want to wait. They did not want to go through with the unpleasantness of time apart to prepare their land. They were determined on their course.

With great misgiving because of the youth of the couple, the kingdom turned out to give the couple a royal wedding. Never had there been a wedding of such fantastical music and presents, happiness and dancing, laughter and games - even for the King and Queen. The people said to themselves, "Ah, well, perhaps their deep love and faithfulness will afford them a buffer against the vagaries of the outside world. If it is so, they may yet live happily after."

The End.

"Some end," thought Nikki. She headed off to take her math final, knowing as she did so, that Tyler would be at home sobering up from the night before when she got back. Their marriage, which had started out so full of promise, was circling the bottom of the drain. Taking a semester final, especially in math, would give her a chance to rest her brain and focus on something outside of her troubles.

"Why can't he just be honest with me? What's so terrible that he has to get drunk all the time? Why does he have to shut me out? Even worse, why is he running away from God?"

Nikki's thoughts whirled like a tornado until she thought she was going to go crazy with anger, grief, bitterness and frustration.

Tyler had no idea where he was or what he was doing. A slow death by drowning in beer had not been his life's first choice. He had just seemed to drift into it. The occasional party after work, and on the weekends when Nikki was out of town, seemed like so much fun. Nikki didn't seem to mind. After a while, Tyler didn't even tell her about them. Of course, you can't drink without smoking. Eventually, getting drunk didn't seem to satisfy anymore, so marijuana and opium began to make an appearance.

Getting high was so relaxing. He could forget everything and everybody. And beer just loosened him up. He and his buddies could laugh for hours over nothing when they got together.

It was possible that Nikki might have objected to his coming home smashed, crashed and doped. Tyler was careful that she didn't find out. Being a good husband was a high standard that he had set for himself in the beginning. It was unbearable that she might find out that he was making such mistakes, that he wasn't the strong and perfect man that he set himself up to be. To him, the tiniest crack in his armor of strong silence was a flaw of earthquake proportions.

The pressure of cheating on Nikki along with the use of drugs and alcohol became too much to handle. Tyler found himself leaving Nikki and returning to Cody that spring. He saw Nikki now and then, when she came looking for him. His heart would tug a bit, but he learned to drown or smoke it out. Mostly he moved from friend to friend, using whenever, wherever and from whomever he could bum the stuff off of. His heart hardened more and more each day.

Stories from the Living Room

During that time, Nikki continued her freshman year at U. W. She found herself immersed in reading her Bible. She had always read, but now it was like a fever within her. She didn't know it was possible to feel so close to God on such a personal level. By continually being brought back to Psalm 51, she realized that sometimes God needs to break us down to rebuild us, and that she wasn't going to be able to drag Tyler back. There wasn't a relationship in the world that could be more important to Tyler than the one he was meant to have with God.

"God, Tyler is Yours. Please do whatever You have to do to bring him back into a relationship with You. Right now I'm willing to let him die if that is what it takes to break him down. I promise to leave Tyler in Your hands now." It was a prayer that Nikki meant down to her toes.

"That truly isn't a safe prayer, Nikki," said Pastor Kenny during one of their counseling sessions. "I've seen people almost die from it."

"That's fine with me," said Nikki. "There isn't any other way for me to pray for him right now. Tyler's down to nothing but skin and bones. He's walking around town with his clothes in a garbage sack. He's miserable and so stubborn that he won't own up to anything. He's going to be one of those people who have to hit rock bottom before they look up and realize that Jesus is the only way."

Kenny agreed it was the right prayer for Tyler.

"I hear your folks would like you to divorce him," said Kenny.

"Yeah," said Nikki. "My brother got drunk a couple of weeks ago and tried to beat him up. My family is really upset with Tyler right now. They all want me to divorce him! I'm not going to though. God is telling me not to go that route."

Classes found Nikki right on schedule with her studies. Every weekend she made the trip back to Cody to stay with her parents and counsel with Pastor Kenny. The weeks went on and Nikki gradually came to terms with her situation. She didn't cry so much. She kept on reading her Bible and praying.

It was the end of that spring semester in April that Tyler finally realized the truth. He was sick, skinny and stupid in his misery. He knew that he loved Nikki, and he had once loved God and all the drugs and alcohol had not been able to delete that from his soul. He knew he wanted Nikki and God back in his life.

"You've been through too much, Tyler," said Pastor Kenny. "You two won't survive together if we don't get God and some structure back into your life. So, this is what we're going to do; you're going to stay with my family and me. You are going to get a job and keep it. You're going to have a Bible reading schedule and we will talk every day about what you are reading. On the weekends, you and Nikki will have marriage counseling together. As you heal and come out of your old habits, we will start to talk about the two of you living with each other."

It was only a month and a half later that Nikki and Tyler got an apartment together in Cody for the summer. They had dealt with many things in their relationship. But even so, they knew that they were hurrying too fast. They were married and wanted to act like it. It was a stormy time for them. Tyler still had a resistance to the daily requirements of a job, especially the getting up and going to it part.

He would still have the occasional beer. Nikki was positive that each and every time he drank he was going to slide all the way back down to the bottom. Drinking was an ugly button to push. Every disagreement was a raging war. They had a lot to work through. Neither one of them had believed that marriage could be so much work.

It was that same summer that Nikki found herself pregnant. It wasn't planned. One can't always plan these things out. Sometimes God has His own agenda. They decided it would be best to stay in Cody for a year near all the people who loved and supported them in their marriage. Tyler worked as a carpenter to support his family, and Nikki attended classes in Powell at Northwest College. Nothing was going to stop her from showing that wizened, old toad of a high school teacher how wrong he was.

Korah arrived right on schedule. She had her momma's looks and her daddy's grin. Nikki and Tyler had been back together for just longer than a year now. It was time for them to consider moving to Laramie to continue Nikki's education.

For the fall semester they went down to Laramie. Their marriage had morphed into a true friendship. Nikki found that the little things didn't matter so much, and Tyler found that supporting his wife and taking care of his little girl satisfied him more than almost anything else could.

He also found that God's call on him was not going to fade away. Every time they moved away from Cody, they found themselves wanting to come back. They now live in Cody. Nikki is teaching in one of the local school systems. Tyler is pursuing his call to ministry.

"We don't have the perfect marriage," says Nikki. "I don't think anyone does, really. The only perfect thing in our lives is God."

"It has been a hard time for us," says Tyler. "Having Korah was a true wake-up call for me. It was time for me to grow up and be a man. My own father was never in my life. I didn't want that for my daughter."

"We don't have a cuddly, cutesy kind of marriage. Enjoying each other doesn't have to be based on that kind of fantasy. As long as God has first place in both of our lives, our marriage works great. It's when we slack off on our Bible reading and/or prayer time that our marriage starts to limp, just a little."

"People look at me kind of funny when I say that," explains Nikki. "It's true, though. I can tell instantly if Tyler has missed even one day of reading and prayer."

"Yeah," says Tyler. "It sounds weird, even to other Christians, but it's serious. Psalm 119:9 says, 'How can a young man keep his way pure? By guarding it according to the Word.' Our testimony isn't about all the grief we've gone through. It isn't about the fantasy world I tried to build around myself. It's about God. He brought us together. He healed us, both individually and as a couple. He called us, her to be a teacher and me into youth ministry."

"God is the only real and sure thing in this world. He is our Guard."

Satan came to steal, kill and destroy me and for a long time I allowed it to happen. I have been saved by grace and delivered from bondage. I have found security, love and abundant life in Jesus. He saved my life.

CONCLUSION

A conclusion per Webster's Dictionary is *a final summation.* How do you summarize these 14 stories. It is very difficult from the perspective of each story individually, so let's not go there. Why make it hard? The easiest way to summarize these stories – this book – is to say that God brought hope to each and every person in the middle of the mess they were in.

God is real. He lives to bring hope to all of us. We are all in need of a relationship with Him. No one needs religion. No one needs another place to go and be judged. We all need the love and acceptance and hope that comes from giving our lives over to God and learning how to live in hope.

When you are in a tunnel convinced that the only light you see is an oncoming train, grab God and hold on. The train might come by fast and the only way you will survive is to hold on to God. If you have no idea how to do that, please call someone who knows the real God. Don't call someone just because they go to church, call someone you can tell knows God. That person will tell you how to grab and hold onto the true living God.

The people in these stories do meet together most Sunday mornings in Cody in the building where Cougar Avenue intersects with 19th Street. Yes, it's a church building, but the people inside will welcome you into their hearts and lives. They will help you find God and hold on tight.

So if you want to, come on by and check it out. If you don't want to come, take time now to talk to God. He's right there where you are and He loves you and cares for you very much. If you would like more information and you have internet access, check out aplaceofhopeonline.com.

For more information on reaching your city with
stories from your church, please contact
Good Catch Publishing at…
www.goodcatchpublishing.com

GOOD CATCH
PUBLISHING